THE
BATTLE
OF
ALTARS

Spiritual Warfare Chronicles Volume II
Foreword: Bishop Tudor Bismarck

THE
BATTLE
OF
ALTARS

Spiritual Technology for Divine Encounters!

Overthrowing evil altars and establishing righteous altars for changing nations!

DR. FRANCIS MYLES

This product is available at special quantity discounts for bulk purchase for sales promotions, premiums, fund-raising, and educational needs. For details, call us at (602) 888-0364 or visit my website at www.francismyles.com

Battle of Altars by Dr. Francis Myles

Published by Dr. Francis Myles and Francis Myles International

950 Eagles Landing Parkway, Unit 618, Stockbridge, Georgia 30281

Visit the authors' websites at francismyles.com

Library of Congress Cataloging-in-Publication Data:

An application to register this book for cataloging has been submitted to the Library of Congress.

International Standard Book Number: 978-1-7327859-4-6
Printed in the United States of America

Contents

Foreword

There are significant leaders that God raises to serve their generation. King David served his generation Acts 13:26, "For David, after he had served his own generation by the will of God, fell on sleep, and was laid unto his fathers, and saw corruption." Leaders that God raises have specific assignments to serve their generation, and for every assignment given, God empowers his servants with the ability and power to achieve God's mandate. God also places unique revelation knowledge and a message for the generation His servants serve.

Dr. Francis Myles has been raised by God to serve this generation. He has an uncanny way of presenting to the world the revelation knowledge God has given him. As a prolific writer, Dr. Francis Myles has penned classics that reshape the "mindset" of the reader and the student. Also, he has brought clarity and direction to the church at large.

"*The Battle of Altars*" is part of a series "Spiritual Warfare Chronicles." In this book, Dr. Myles' systematic, methodical mind is on display at its very best. He carefully and meticulously crafts the art and the science of "Spiritual Warfare." Prayer is an essential part of a believer's walk with God, but "Spiritual Warfare" is an art in the discipline of prayer that can be taught and learned.

"*The Battle of Altars*" captures both the mindset and application of prayer to breakdown demonic altars and establish pure Godly Altars. This level of spiritual encounter is for the mature believer. However, a novice can be taught and trained to become proficient in deep spiritual warfare encounters. Dr.

Myles establishes that a believer can build Godly altars through methodical disciplined prayer.

Finally, Dr. Myles tracks the journey of altars Biblically, historically, and culturally. He shows how through the cross of Jesus Christ, diabolical satanic altars can be neutralized, broken, and destroyed. That through the finished work of Jesus, we as believers can raise Godly altars to gain continual victories over Satan and his demonic systems. *The Battle of Altars* is a significant work of art that empowers God's people in the earth to deal with 21st Century challenges.

This generation faces spiritual warfare on a level that no previous generation has faced. Paul told Timothy that the last days would be characterized and shaped by seducing spirits and doctrines of devils. 1 Timothy 4:1, *"Now the Spirit speaks expressly, that in the latter times some shall depart from the faith, giving heed to seducing spirits, and doctrines of devils."* The Battle of Altars provides the necessary and essential tools for 21st-century spiritual altars.

On a personal note, I'd like to thank Dr. Francis Myles for continuing to craft books that add so much value to the Body of Christ. I'd like to congratulate him on this, another master class book. I pray God's best on him, his family, and his global ministry.

Sincerely,

Bishop Tudor Bismark
Jabula New Life Ministries International
Harare, Zimbabwe

Preface

For our struggle is not against flesh and blood [contending only with physical opponents], but against the rulers, against the powers, against the world forces of this [present] darkness, against the spiritual forces of wickedness in the heavenly (supernatural) places.

Ephesians 6:12 (AMP)

For we wrestle not against flesh and blood, but against principalities, against powers, against the rulers of the darkness of this world, against spiritual wickedness in high places.

Ephesians 6:12 (KJV)

The Bible does not hide the fact that we are involved in high-stakes warfare for the souls of men and the future of planet Earth. Apostle Paul, in the book of Ephesians, takes us behind the veil of the flesh (this body of sin that we all share) and unmasks both the nature of this war and the evil entities behind it. The Apostle Paul lets us know that this "war" is spiritual in nature and its battle dynamics.

According to Ephesians 6:12, this "struggle or warfare" is not *"against flesh and blood but against principalities, against powers, against the rulers of the darkness of this world, against spiritual wickedness in high places."* In other words, you don't cross the line into the yard of a notorious neighbor and initiate a fistfight and then call it "spiritual warfare!" In the penal code of most law-abiding nations, your actions would fall under the statutes, which condemn trespassing and physical assault. In such a scenario, your notorious and annoying neighbor would have legal standing to call the police to arrest you.

Knowing that some Christians would be tempted to fight a "spiritual war" with physical means, Saint Paul goes out of his way to emphasize the fact that we are not "fighting with flesh and blood" (humans). But we are in a serious spiritual wrestling match with celestial beings (fallen angels) that are fighting against us in a well-organized hierarchal order. The Apostle Paul lists the hierarchal order or ranking of these evil spiritual beings that we are fighting, namely:

1. *"Principalities."* Principalities are the highest-ranking celestial beings (fallen angels) in Satan's kingdom. As their ranking suggests, they are the ones Satan uses as "ruling spirits" over each nation on earth. When Daniel was praying and fasting for 21 days (Daniel 10), the angel God sent to bring him the answer told him that he had been delayed for 21 days because of spiritual resistance from the Prince of Persia. The Prince of Persia was the demonic principality over the Persian empire that Daniel was living and serving under at the time.

2. *"Powers."* As the name and ranking suggest, Powers are celestial beings (fallen angels) in Satan's kingdom who are responsible for manifesting the spiritual power behind many "signs, wonders, and miracles" performed by those engaged in the occult. They are performed by human messengers of Satan, such as witches, magicians, necromancers, sorcerers, or psychics, just to name a few. "Powers" were the demonic entities behind Jannis and Jambres, who opposed Moses in Exodus 7:10-12 by creating their own snakes just like Moses had done by God's command. Moses' snake swallowed the two snakes created by these two Egyptian magicians, whom the book Jasher says

were the two sons of Balaam, the soothsayer alluded to in the book of Numbers.

3. *"Rulers of the darkness of this world."* The "rulers of the darkness of this world" are celestial beings (fallen angels) in Satan's kingdom who influence the minds of men and women by using vain philosophies (ways of thinking, such as Marxism, Communism, Socialism, Atheism). That makes it difficult for humans to "see" the glorious light of the gospel of Jesus Christ. Saint Paul in 2 Corinthians 4:3-4 describes the work of these demonic entities this way, *"But even if our gospel is [in some sense] hidden [behind a veil], it is hidden [only] to those who are perishing; ⁴ among them the god of this world [Satan] has blinded the minds of the unbelieving to prevent them from seeing the illuminating light of the gospel of the glory of Christ, who is the image of God."*

4. *"Spiritual wickedness in high places."* "Spiritual wickedness in high places" is the fourth-ranking of Satanic angelic beings, who are the ones who are behind the warfare described in this book, *"The Battle of Altars."* As the name *"Spiritual wickedness in high places"* suggests, these fallen angels are responsible for deceiving humans into building or erecting "evil altars." They are responsible for projecting every form of spiritual wickedness from spiritual platforms the Bible calls "altars." In the Bible, most "altars" were erected or built on high points of elevation, geographically speaking; thus, they became widely known as "high places" as 1 Kings 11 suggests.

For when Solomon was old, his wives turned his heart away after other gods; and his heart was not completely devoted to the Lord his God, as was the heart of his father David. ⁵ For Solomon went after Ashtoreth, the [fertility] goddess of the Sidonians, and after Milcom the horror (detestable idol) of the Ammonites. ⁶ Solomon did evil [things] in the sight of the Lord, and did not follow the Lord fully, as his father David had done. ⁷ Then Solomon built a high place for [worshiping] Chemosh the horror (detestable idol) of Moab, on the hill which is east of Jerusalem, and for Molech the horror (detestable idol) of the sons of Ammon. [8] *And he did the same for all of his foreign wives, who burned incense and sacrificed to their gods.*

(1 Kings 11:4-8)

It's so sad and tragic that Solomon, whom God made "the wisest and richest man who has ever lived," died an idol worshipper. Using Solomon's lustful desire for foreign women, Satan used him to teach the nation of Israel how to build or erect "high places" (altars) dedicated to demonic deities. Please take note of the fact that the Bible says, *"Then Solomon built a high place for [worshiping] Chemosh the horror (detestable idol) of Moab, on the hill which is east of Jerusalem, and for Molech the horror (detestable idol) of the sons of Ammon."* The term "high place" is the biblical reference to the evil altars that Solomon built for his idol-worshipping foreign wives. Most importantly, the Bible says that Solomon built these "evil altars" on *"the hill which is east of Jerusalem."* "On the hill" is a direct reference to the fact these altars were geographically positioned on a natural point of elevation. This elevation caused people or worshippers at these altars (high places) to look up to the demonic deity's idol or image being worshipped.

From the testimony of scripture, it seems that Satan's hierarchal kingdom depends on spiritual portals opened by these high places to seduce generations of men into accepting Satan's rule over their lives. That makes the work of *"spiritual wickedness in high places"* extremely important to Satan's kingdom of darkness. Under Satan's hierarchical order of fallen angels, there is a final and lower order consisting of demons (disembodied spirits) and Satan's wicked human agents. They play the role of "foot soldiers" in Satan's march toward global domination. Some of these demons function as "alter egos" to influence millions of people using the earthly platforms of iconic figures or celebrities. In *"The Battle of Altars: Spiritual Technology for Divine Encounters,"* I take you into the world of righteous and evil altars with such forensic aptitude; no stone is left unturned. You will come out of this journey with practical tools for winning the *"The Battle of Altars"* in your life and ministry!

Yours for Messiah's Kingdom,

Dr. Francis Myles
Co-Author of "Idols Riot!"

Spiritual warfare is a battle of altars.

1

The Battle of Altars

The Philistines brought the Ark of God from Ebenezer to Ashdod. They took the Ark of God into the house of Dagon and set it beside Dagon [their idol]. When they of Ashdod arose early on the morrow, behold, Dagon had fallen upon his face on the ground before the ark of the Lord. So, they took Dagon and set him in his place again. (1 Samuel 5:1-3)

What most of us call spiritual warfare is nothing short of the battle of altars. Once you understand the spiritual technology behind altars and that they are places of exchange, you will quickly realize there can be no warfare or divine confrontation between spiritual entities from the Kingdom of God and the kingdom of darkness without standing on an altar! Any form of spiritual warfare on earth that is not connected to an altar is illegal since altars are the only legal means for spirit beings from both kingdoms to land on earth. In a later chapter, we will examine the 12 Laws of Altars that will shed more light on the spiritual dynamics of altars. Without a doubt, altars are spiritual platforms for effecting spiritual encounters between humanity and divinity! That is why when God meets with a man, an altar is born! In similar and copy-cat fashion, when Satan meets with a man, an evil altar is also born.

When people carrying righteous altars collide with people who carry evil, demonically engineered altars, a spiritual battle ensues. We call this spiritual warfare when, in essence, it is a battle of altars. Hence, the name of this chapter (and the book). In the above passage of Scripture, we have an interesting case study that showcases the working of this powerful principle of spiritual warfare.

The Ark of God: A Superior Altar

In 1 Samuel 1:4, the Philistines managed to capture the Ark of God in a battle with the children of Israel due to the sinful lifestyle of Eli's two sons, Hophni and Phinehas.

> So, the people sent word to Shiloh, and from there they carried the ark of the covenant of the LORD of hosts who sits above the cherubim; and the two sons of Eli, Hophni and Phinehas, were with the ark of the covenant of God. So it happened that as the ark of the covenant of the LORD came into the camp, all [the people of] Israel shouted with a great shout, and the earth resounded. When the Philistines heard the noise of the shout, they said, "What does the noise of this great shout in the camp of the Hebrews mean?" Then they understood that the ark of the LORD had come into the camp. The Philistines were afraid, for they said, "God has come into the camp." And they said, "Woe [disaster is coming] to us! For nothing like this has happened before.
>
> (1 Samuel 4:4-7)

Perhaps there was no article of God's temple that was more sacred in the Levitical priesthood than the Ark of God. The Ark of God, also referred to as the Ark of the Covenant, was one of the most powerful symbols of faith and God's presence in the entire Old Testament. The Ark of the Covenant was a box of acacia wood overlaid with gold both inside and out. Hebrews 9:4 states that the Ark contained "the golden pot that had manna, and Aaron's rod that budded, and the tablets of the covenant." Two angelic Cherubim statues sat on top of this divine mercy seat. Everything inside the Ark of God was supernatural: the manna that fell from heaven was given to sustain the children of Israel supernaturally. Not to mention Aaron's priestly Rod of Authority that budded supernaturally violated the laws of nature. Then there were the tablets of stone that were given to the Prophet Moses on Mount Sinai on which God wrote the Ten Commandments with His finger.

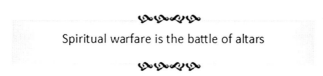

Spiritual warfare is the battle of altars

No wonder there was no earthly altar that could compete with the Ark of God. The Ark of God was truly a lofty altar in Israel. That is why, when Joshua and the people of Israel were crossing the river Jordan to take the city of Jericho, God instructed him to tell the Levites to go ahead of the people while carrying the Ark of God. When the Levites ' feet stepped in the River Jordan while carrying the Ark of God, something supernatural happened. The water of the River Jordan began to part to allow the childr en of Israel to pass through. From this act, people in all the Gentile nations, including Jericho, knew the power of the Ark of God. Even the prostitute Rahab told the spies that Joshua sent, "all the inhabitants of the land faint because of you." (Joshua 2:9)

Devil, Step Aside!

> *And when those who were carrying the Ark came up to the Jordan, and the feet of the priests carrying the ark were submerged at the edge of the water (for the Jordan overflows all of its banks throughout the time of harvest), the waters which were flowing down from above stopped and rose up in one mass a great distance away at Adam, the city that is beside Zarethan.*
>
> *(Joshua 3:15-16)*

Interestingly enough, the Bible says that the River Jordan's water parted all the way back to the city of Adam. This Scripture passage exposes two powerful redeeming principles that I want to address regarding the power of a righteous altar.

First, all that ails the human race can be traced back to the first Adam and his catastrophic fall in the Garden of Eden because he failed to prioritize God over his wife. In the Garden of Eden, Adam essentially idolized his wife and unknowingly built an evil altar in his heart on which he set her in the stead of God. So, in essence, the fall of man is not only connected to rebellion to God's authority but also plain idolatry and the erecting of an evil altar in Adam's soul. That is why understanding the subject of altars is critical to maintaining a life of sustained breakthrough in God's Kingdom.

Second, this passage shows us that when we are standing on a righteous altar – a superior altar, so to speak – we can step in the muddy waters of our ancestral bloodlines and reverse every generational curse that has ever existed in them, all the way back to the first Adam. Standing on a righteous and superior altar, we can move and turn back the tide of idolatrous spirits, iniquities, and all the evil altars that Satan ever planted in our ancestral bloodlines. That is precisely what the Lord Jesus Christ did because He gave His life for us on the superior altar of Calvary. Jesus pushed back the tide of sin and iniquity in all human bloodlines, all the way back to the fall of the first Adam. He essentially reversed the curse of separation of fallen man from God. 1 Corinthians 15:22 says, *"For just as in Adam all die, so also in Christ all will be made alive."*

The Ark of God is Captured!

The messenger replied, "Israel has fled before the Philistines and there has also been a great slaughter among the people. Also your two sons, Hophni and Phinehas, are dead, and the ark of God has been taken." When he mentioned the ark of God, Eli fell off the seat backwards by the side of the [city] gate. His neck was broken and he died, for he was old and heavy. He had judged Israel for forty years. Now his daughter-in-law, Phinehas' wife, was pregnant, and was about to give birth; so when she heard the news that the ark of God had been taken and that her father-in-law and her husband had died, she kneeled down and gave birth, because her [labor] pains began. And about the time of her death [following the sudden birth] the women attending her said to her, "Do not be afraid, for you have given birth to a son." But she did not answer

or pay any attention. And she named the boy [b]Ichabod, saying, "The glory
has left Israel," because the ark of God had been taken and because of [the
deaths of] her father-in-law and her husband. She said, "The glory has left
Israel, for the ark of God has been taken.

(1 Samuel 4:17-22)

Knowing that spiritual warfare comes down to the battle of altars, the capture of the Ark of God by the Philistines was no small thing. It was seriously terrifying! The capture of the Ark of God meant that Israel was exposed, and every other gentile nation that feared them because of the Ark of God would be emboldened to attack them. Most importantly, the loss of the Ark of God to the Philistines meant that God's glory, which was connected to the Ark of God, had also departed from Israel. This was frightening news. The Bible says once the news reached Eli's ears, the High Priest, he fell and broke his neck. In the meantime, Phinehas' pregnant wife, when she heard the dreadful news that the Ark of God had been captured, went into untimely labor and began to give birth to a son. While she was dying in childbirth, she named her newborn baby boy "Ichabod." The term "Ichabod" literally means "the glory had departed from Israel!"

The million-dollar question is, Why did God allow the Ark of God to be captured by the Philistines? I believe it was to teach us an object lesson. Namely, "the glory of God does not travel on the shoulders of filthy and unrighteous servants of God."

I've met many ministers of the gospel who were mightily used by God at one time or another. But when I met them, I quickly realized that they were old shells of what they used to be. God's glory that they used to carry had already departed from their lives and ministries. It was clear to me within moments of meeting them that they were not standing on the same superior altar that made them shake nations and manifest mighty signs, wonders, and miracles. Why? Because "the glory of God does not travel on the shoulders of filthy and unrighteous servants of God."

The two sons of Eli, who brought the Ark of God into the battlefield, had very corrupt lifestyles. They were serial thieves and fornicators who brought the entire priesthood of Levi into great disrepute. Their evil lifestyles caused some of the faithful to stumble and brought confusion to others in Israel. Consequently, they had already lost the favor of His presence long before they brought the Ark of God into the battlefield. It is difficult to overthrow an evil altar with which you have "something in common." The two sons of Eli had things in common with the Philistines. Consequently, God could not use them to deliver Israel. Instead, the Philistines' evil altars took the day, and the Ark of God was captured! What a shame!

Altars are Platforms of Warfare

Woe to us! Who will rescue us from the hand of these mighty gods? These are the gods who struck the Egyptians with all kinds of plagues in the wilderness.

(1 Samuel 4:8)

Whatever you think of the Philistines, you must at least admit that they had more fear and reverence for the Ark of God than the two sons of Eli who were carrying the Ark of God. What is of note is that when the Philistines heard the thunderous noise of the children of Israel as the Ark of God entered the battlefield, they said to themselves, "Woe to us!" They knew that they were doomed because they recognized that the Ark of God was the most powerful platform for waging war. They had seen the Ark of God in action in previous battles. They knew what the Ark of God did to the flooded River Jordan and what it did to the ancient and impenetrable City of Jericho.

They had seen how the Ark of God decimated stronger and mightier nations than theirs when it entered the battlefield on the shoulders of righteous men like Moses and Joshua. So, they went into battle expecting to lose. Imagine their surprise when they easily vanquished Israel and captured the most sacred artifact in the Temple of God. What's undeniable is that even the enemy recognized that the Ark of God was a superior altar compared to any altar in Philistia. The Philistines recognized that an altar, such as the Ark of God, is a spiritual platform for the launching of warfare. Consequently, the most important thing I want you to remember is that "altars are platforms of warfare!" You cannot wage an effective campaign of spiritual warfare if you're not standing on an altar! It's actually impossible! The Body of Christ must understand this very powerful spiritual technology that God has given us for advancing His Kingdom.

Two Opposing Altars

Then the Philistines took the ark of God, and they brought it from Ebenezer to Ashdod. ²They took the ark of God and brought it into the house of Dagon and set it beside [the image of] Dagon [their chief idol]. 3 When the people of Ashdod got up early the next day, behold, Dagon had fallen on his face on the ground before the ark of the Lord. So, they took Dagon and returned him to his place.

(1 Samuel 5:1-3)

We have already stated that the Ark of God was a symbol of God's abiding presence in Israel. Without a doubt, the Ark of God was a mobile altar that traveled with the children of Israel wherever they went. The Bible tells us that the Philistines brought the Ark of God to the city of Ashdod. What follows is truly interesting in the study of spiritual warfare, especially the battle of altars. I am certain every follower of Messiah Jesus knows that the Bible says we are involved in high-stakes spiritual warfare between the Kingdom of Light and the forces of darkness.

The Lord recently showed me that what we call spiritual warfare is nothing short of the spiritual battle that ensues when an altar from God's Kingdom of Light is placed next to an altar from the kingdom of darkness. The close proximity of these spiritual power stations and the fact that no two altars can occupy the same space result in spiritual warfare. Maybe you ever wondered why some people at your new job displayed a passionate animosity towards you even though you were meeting them for the very first time? I assure you, it's not personal. The answer lies in understanding the dynamics of spiritual altars. Whenever two individuals carrying two opposing altars come into contact, the spirit of animosity between them is proof that their two altars are now engaged in a spiritual battle.

In the above passage of scripture, the Philistines brought the Ark of God from Ebenezer to Ashdod. Upon their arrival, they took the Ark of God into the house of Dagon, their most powerful deity. They set the Ark of the God of Israel next to this worthless idol.

According to Wikipedia, "Dagon or Dagan is an ancient Mesopotamian and ancient Canaanite deity. He appears to have been worshipped as a fertility god in Ebla, Assyria, Ugarit, and among the Amorites. The Hebrew Bible mentions him as the national god of the Philistines."

When they woke up the following morning, Dagon was lying on the floor with his face kissing the ground. The Ark of God, which was the altar of the Lord God of Israel, had quickly pronounced its supremacy over the Philistines' idol. Have you ever wondered why some people rub your spirit the wrong way, even when they are offering you a pleasant smile? You could be discerning the evil altar in their soul that is fighting against the altar of the Lord in your soul. Unfortunately, this same phenomenon occurs between the bloodlines of believers who love the Lord Jesus but have evil altars in their family bloodline that have never been torn down. This book contains a divine prescription for deliverance from the oppressive power of these evil altars.

The Superior Altar Always Takes the Day!

But when they arose early the next morning, behold, Dagon had again fallen on his face on the ground before the ark of the Lord, and [his] head and both the palms of his hands were lying cut off on the threshold; only the trunk of Dagon was left him. [5] This is the reason neither the priests of Dagon nor any who come into Dagon's house tread on the threshold of Dagon in Ashdod to this day. [6] But the hand of the Lord was heavy upon the people of Ashdod, and He caused [mice to spring up and there was] very deadly destruction and He smote the people with [very painful] tumors or boils, both Ashdod and its territory. [7] When the men of Ashdod saw that it was so, they said, The ark of the God of Israel must not remain with us, for His hand is heavy on us and on Dagon our god.

(1 Samuel 5:4-7)

No two altars can occupy the same space!

According to the 12 Law of Altars, whoever carries the superior altar in the spirit takes the day! What does this statement mean? It means that to be delivered from the power of an evil altar and the idol (demon-god) connected to it, we must strengthen the altar of the LORD in our life. The altar of the Lord in our life must become stronger than the idol and evil altar we are trying to destroy. The good news is that when we use prayers that appeal to the Courts of Heaven, we automatically gain the spiritual stature of the Courts of Heaven. The Courts of Heaven function above the evil powers of every evil altar. In the above passage of Scripture, when the Philistines brought the Ark of God into the house of Dagon, they did not understand the 12th Law of Altars. But God did!

God did not waste time demonstrating to them in no uncertain terms that the altar of the Ark of God was superior to the altar of the idol (Dagon). When the Philistines found Dagon lying prostrate before the Ark of God, they did not get the message. So, they propped up this worthless demon-god once more and set it next to the Ark of God. It was a huge mistake! The second day when they returned, the image of the idol, Dagon, was lying on the floor. It's head, and the palms of its hands were broken beyond repair. This time the Philistines got the message, and they were terrified because Dagon was their most powerful national deity!

The moral of the story is abundantly clear. Whoever carries the superior altar takes the day! So, if you want the LORD to deliver you from the power of the idols and evil altars erected in your soul or generational bloodline, you must make sure that you practice spiritual disciplines like praying and fasting.

Regular times of prayer and fasting will starve these idols and evil altars in your soul or bloodline. Fasting does not change God, but it does strengthen your spirit man!

For instance, if the altar of sexual perversion in your life is stronger than the altar of sanctification, you will lose the fight for holiness to the devil. That explains why a person, used mightily by God, can fall prey to the scourge of sexual scandal. That does not mean that these believers (including King David), who fell into sexual sin, were not saved. Most important, it does not mean they did not love Jesus. It simply means that they failed to destroy the idol and evil altar of sexual perversion rooted in either their soul or ancestral bloodline. Unfortunately for them, the stronger altar of sexual pervasion took the day, taking their reputation and famous worldwide ministries with it!

Whoever has the superior altar rules the day!

PRAYER OF ACTIVATION!

"Heavenly Father, I ask for the Court of Heaven to be seated and for the books of my destiny to be opened as I come before the Judge of all the earth to plead my case against any evil altar in my life or bloodline that is speaking against me. I decree and declare that the Holy Spirit is my official guide and counselor in this courtroom. Heavenly Father, I surrender all rights to self-representation; instead, I ask my defense attorney and mediator of the new covenant, the Lord Jesus Christ, to represent me in your Royal Courtroom against all idols and evil altars that are controlling my life and bloodline in any way. I also ask the Lord Jesus to heal me by His blood from all soul wounds caused by idols and evil altars in my bloodline. I am seeking a verdict of release from the power of these evil altars, in Jesus' Name.

I now enter a plea of 'guilty' into the court's records concerning any legitimate accusations that Satan has filed in court against me or my bloodline. For Jesus said, in Matthew 5:25, *"Come to terms quickly [at the earliest opportunity] with your opponent at law while you are with him on the way [to court], so that your opponent does not hand you over to the judge, and the judge to the guard, and you are thrown into prison."* Lord, since I am under oath, I cannot lie about my sinful activities and the iniquities of my bloodline that are connected to idolatry and the erecting evil altars. I repent for all sins and transgressions that I and my ancestors ever committed against you and the laws of nature. Cleanse me from all sin by the blood of Jesus, according to 1 John 1:9. I now formally submit my guilty plea and repentance to the court, in Jesus' name."

Heavenly Father,

- I decree and declare that the Ark of God in my life will never ever be captured by the demonic powers.
- I decree and declare that as a carrier of the Ark of God, I contain the superior altar to the evil altars in my bloodline, in Jesus Name.
- I decree and declare that all opposing and evil altars against me are destroyed in Jesus' Name.
- I decree and declare that I am completely healed from all soul wounds that I have in common with any evil altar in my bloodline, in Jesus' Name.
- I decree and declare that I am a victor in the battle of altars in my bloodline in Jesus' Name.

LIFE APPLICATION

SECTION

Memory Verse

The Philistines brought the ark of God from Ebenezer to Ashdod. 2 They took the ark of God into the house of Dagon and set it beside Dagon [their idol]. 3 When they of Ashdod arose early on the morrow, behold, Dagon had fallen upon his face on the ground before the ark of the Lord. So, they took Dagon and set him in his place again.

(1 Samuel 5:1-2)

Reflections

1. What is the battle of altars?

The battle between the altar that was born when I met God + the evil altar that the enemy set up. Otherwise, it is also known as spiritual warfare.

2. What happens when two opposing altars are placed next to each other?

a spiritual battle occurs between good + evil.

2

Altars & The Law of Dominion

The heaven, even the heavens, are the Lord's; But the earth He has given to the children of men.

(Psalms 115:16, NKJV)

The most significant discovery in life is the discovery of purpose – most important, God's purpose. The late Dr. Myles Munroe declared, "Wherever purpose is not known, abuse is inevitable."

The genesis of God's purpose for creating the human race can be found in the first two chapters of Genesis. The Genesis account underscores God's inherent motivation to create a physical planet called Earth and create spirit-children that He collectively called "Adam." God then created physical bodies made of dirt to house these spirit-beings so that they could become legal residents and guardians of the visible world. From the beginning, our physical world (earth) was designed to be a spiritual colony of the Kingdom of Heaven. It was never designed to be a habitation of demons and every foul spirit.

Then God said:

"Let Us make man in Our image, according to Our likeness; let them have dominion over the fish of the sea, over the birds of the air, and over the cattle, over all the earth and over every creeping thing that creeps on the earth." So God created man in His own image; in the image of God He created him; male and female He created them. Then God blessed them, and God said to them, "Be fruitful and multiply; fill the earth and subdue it; have dominion over the fish of the sea, over the birds of the air, and over every living thing that moves on the earth"

(Genesis 1:26-28, NKJV)

Colonization: God's Big Idea

In Genesis 1:26-28, we are told that humans were created by God to be ambassadorial representatives of God's invisible Kingdom on the visible planet, called Earth. God's big idea was to colonize earth by making it a colony of His Heavenly Kingdom. Said simply, humans were created to rule or exercise dominion over the world of matter on behalf of God's invisible Kingdom. Consequently, our purpose on earth is intricately tied to fulfilling our prophetic assignment as official representatives of the Kingdom of God. Anything short of fulfilling our ambassadorial assignment of manifesting the Kingdom of God here on earth as it is in heaven is a gross violation of our purpose. We were created to manifest God's character and His Kingdom government. Going to church becomes religion at the point we deviate from manifesting our Kingdom ambassadorship.

Our Dominion Mandate

So, God created man in His own image; in the image of God He created him; male and female He created them. Then God blessed them, and God said to them, "Be fruitful and multiply; fill the earth and subdue it; have dominion over the fish of the sea, over the birds of the air, and over every living thing that moves on the earth"

(Genesis 1:27-28 NKJV).

On the sixth day of creation, God created His master species, mankind! Created in both the image (God's spiritual essence) and likeness (God's DNA) of God, there was no other creature that could compete with man's unique position as the manifest son of God here on earth. However, it's the gift of dominion that God gave mankind that is of interest. It's the one that ties us directly to the subject of altars and why they are so critical to the economy of God.

In Genesis 1:26, God said, "Let them have dominion," which comes from the Hebrew word "Mamlakah," which means "ruler, rulership or kingdom." According to God, this dominion mandate upon mankind would rest on four pillars. I call these pillars "the pillars of dominion."

1. Being fruitful
2. Multiplying
3. Filling or Replenishing the Earth
4. Subduing the Earth

These four pillars of dominion are interlinked. First, being "fruitful" suggests that God created mankind as a walking "warehouse of seed." This means no human being was born "empty," whether they discover their seed bag or not. Their seed bag contains the seeds of dominion. However, in this chapter, I will show you that these four pillars of dominion are connected by a tabletop called an altar, which binds them together while serving as an interface between our world and the supernatural world.

The Implications of Our Dominion Mandate

Then God said, "Let Us make man in Our image, according to Our likeness; let them have dominion over the fish of the sea, over the birds of the air, and over the cattle, over all the earth and over every creeping thing that creeps on the earth.

(Genesis 1:26)

The million-dollar question I want you to ask yourself is, "What is the spiritual connection between the subject of altars and man's dominion mandate?" When God created Adam and Eve (the first humans) and gave them dominion over this planet, He made an irreversible decree that would impact God and every celestial being (spirit) in all creation in a significant manner. When God transferred dominion (rulership) of this planet to mankind, He deliberately excluded Himself and every celestial (angelic) being from the earth's legal authority structure.

When God said, "Let them" have dominion, everything shifted on earth! Please take note of the words "Let them." God was not drunk when He issued these words! Take note that this expression excludes God, angels, or any spirit being, from interfering in earthly affairs without the legal permission of a man. By using the expression "let them," God locked Himself out of influencing this world without man's permission. Why would He do such a thing? Two primary reasons:

1. God wanted His spirit-children housed in bodies of dirt (humus) to rule and subdue the earth as kings and priests and ambassadors of His invisible Kingdom on our visible planet.
2. In His eternal love for us, God knew at the time of Adam's creation that Lucifer and one-third of His angels had already fallen from grace and were cast out of heaven. Being a loving Father, God did not want these fallen and malicious spirits to rule the planet He created for mankind to rule. So, in His divine providence, God locked them out of our world, but He never threw away the keys to the kingdom of men.

God simply placed the keys to "loose" (allow legal entry) or "bind" (deny access) in our hands. This is exactly what Jesus was referencing when He said in Matthew 18:18, *"I assure you and most solemnly say to you, whatever you bind [forbid, declare to be improper and unlawful] on earth shall have [already] been bound in heaven, and whatever you loose [permit, declare lawful] on earth shall have [already] been loosed in heaven."* This verse means precisely what it says in its literal sense. Heaven can only bind in heaven what man has already bound on earth. This passage from Matthew's gospel is also known as the "Law of Territory." One of the definitions of the Law of Territory (also known as the Law of Dominion) is, "Man was given territorial and stewardship authority over the planet earth." That is still true even though Adam's sin in the Garden of Eden made Satan the de-facto god of this world. King David fraternizes with the Law of Territory in Psalms 115:16 when he says, "The heavens are the heavens of the Lord, But the earth He has given to the children of men."

Man was given territorial and stewardship authority over the planet Earth.

God, Idols, and Altars

For as I passed along and carefully observed your objects of worship, I came also upon an altar with this inscription, To the unknown god. Now what you are already worshiping as unknown, this I set forth to you. ²⁴ The God Who produced and formed the world and all things in it, being Lord of heaven and earth, does not dwell in handmade shrines. ²⁵ Neither is He served by human hands, as though He lacked anything, for it is He Himself Who gives life and breath and all things to all [people].

(Acts 17:23-24)

Since God had effectively and irrevocably locked Himself and all celestial beings out of the Earth's legal authority structure in Genesis 1:26, how was He to get involved in the affairs of men? Like any good and loving parent, God did not create us (give birth to us) and then shrug His shoulders and say, "Well, you are on your own now; I am leaving." God created us first and foremost for intimate fellowship and then to dominate or control this planet on His behalf so

Earth can become a colony of the Kingdom of Heaven. However, by the "Law of Dominion," God could only accomplish both by securing man's permission or cooperation.

The other definition of the Law of Dominion (also known as the Law of Territory) states that "spirits without physical bodies of dirt are illegal on earth" unless they function through a human. That is an unbreakable law of God's Kingdom. Suddenly, prayer becomes critically essential because it becomes man's way of giving God the legal permission He needs to righteously interfere in men's affairs. Essentially, the Law of Dominion transformed the earth into a "world of men." That is why the Messiah had to become a man in order to rescue us legally from the law of sin and death.

As a result of the far-reaching implications of the Law of Dominion, God, in His eternal genius, devised a way for Himself and His holy angels to legally enter our physical planet. God showed Adam how to build a supernatural interface between heaven and earth called an altar. This transpired when He killed an animal in the garden of Eden to atone for their sin, "The Lord God made tunics of [animal] skins for Adam and his wife and clothed them" (Genesis 3:21). How else did the children of Adam & Eve, namely Cain and Abel, know how to build an altar (a spiritual platform for divine encounter) in the fourth chapter of Genesis? The altar, like an airport, would serve as a landing place where divinity meets humanity. It would serve as a consecrated place where spirits can legally land at man's beckoning. Since the first altar in the Garden of Eden was covered in the blood of atonement, the altar would essentially become a place of death, sacrifice, and redemption.

The altar would effectively function as a power-station connecting two worlds – heaven and earth, or hell and earth! Since mankind is the legal guardian of this planet, the most important element at any altar is the man who attends to the altar. The person who serves as the attendant to the altar becomes the servant of God, or the demonic entity, which has been given legal authority to operate freely in the world of men through a dedicated altar. Since there is only One God, any other entity from the kingdom of darkness that is given legal authority through an altar to operate in the world of men becomes the "idol" (demon-god) behind such altars. Since all altars are essentially power stations, the attendant to the altar becomes supernaturally empowered by God or the idol (demon-god) behind the altar. Until the altar is demolished, God, or the demon-gods behind the altar will continue to operate freely in the world of men. This is essentially the spiritual connection between God, idols, and altars! We will explain altars and how they function more thoroughly in later chapters.

PRAYER OF ACTIVATION!

"Heavenly Father, I ask for the Court of Heaven to be seated and for the books of my destiny to be opened as I come before the Judge of all the earth to plead my case against any evil altar in my life or bloodline that is speaking against me. I decree and declare that the Holy Spirit is my official guide and counselor in this courtroom. Heavenly Father, I surrender all rights to self-representation; instead, I ask my defense attorney and mediator of the new covenant, the Lord Jesus Christ, to represent me in your Royal Courtroom against all idols and evil altars that are controlling my life and bloodline, in any way. I also ask the Lord Jesus to heal me by His blood from all soul wounds caused by idols and evil altars in my bloodline. I am seeking a verdict of release from the power of these evil altars, in Jesus' name.

I now enter a plea of 'guilty' into the court's records concerning any legitimate accusations that Satan has filed in Court against me or my bloodline. For Jesus said, in Matthew 5:25, *"Come to terms quickly [at the earliest opportunity] with your opponent at law while you are with him on the way [to court], so that your opponent does not hand you over to the judge, and the judge to the guard, and you are thrown into prison."* Lord, since I am under oath, I cannot lie about my sinful activities and the iniquities of my bloodline that are connected to idolatry and the erecting evil altars. I repent for all sins and transgressions that I and my ancestors ever committed against you and the laws of nature. Cleanse me from all sin by the blood of Jesus, according to 1 John 1:9. I now formally submit my guilty plea and repentance to the court in Jesus' Name."

Heavenly Father,

- I decree and declare that the spirit of dominion is restored over my life!
- I decree and declare that I will walk in dominion over every evil altar in my bloodline, in Jesus' Name!
- I decree and declare that spirits without bodies are illegal on the earth, so I cast out every evil spirit assigned against me in Jesus' Name!
- I decree and declare that I will build righteous altars in my life to release God's supernatural power and presence, in Jesus' Name!
- I take dominion over every evil altar that Satan ever planted in my generational bloodline in Jesus' Name!
- I decree and declare that I am a victor in the battle of altars in my life and bloodline in Jesus' Name!

LIFE APPLICATION

SECTION

Memory Verse

"I assure you and most solemnly say to you, whatever you bind [forbid, declare to be improper and unlawful] on earth shall have [already] been bound in heaven, and whatever you loose [permit, declare lawful] on earth shall have [already] been loosed in heaven."

(Matthew 18:18)

Reflections

1. What is the law of dominion?

   <u>The ability to rule + subdue the</u>
   <u>earth as kings + priests + ambassadors</u>
   <u>of His Kingdom on earth.</u>

2. Why does the law of dominion affect God and demon spirits?

3

Defining An Altar

And Noah built an altar to the Lord and took of every clean [four-footed] animal and of every clean fowl or bird and offered burnt offerings on the altar. [21] When the Lord smelled the pleasing odor [a scent of satisfaction to His heart], the Lord said to Himself, I will never again curse the ground because of man, for the imagination (the strong desire) of man's heart is evil and wicked from his youth; neither will I ever again smite and destroy every living thing, as I have done.

(Genesis 8:20-21)

*B*eing that the subject of altars is central to the whole process of enabling God to interfere legally in the world of men, let us first begin by defining what an altar is from a biblical and Kingdom perspective. It is difficult to understand and master anything that we cannot correctly define and quantify. So here we go!

DEFINITION: *An altar is a supernatural landing strip, a power station, a consecrated place, a place of exchange, a place of sacrifice, a table of fellowship, a place where covenants are made and sustained; it's a spiritual platform where spirits (God, angels, or demons) land; it is where humanity meets with divinity! An altar is also a system of authorization for promises, vows, and agreements between divinity and humanity! In modern language, an altar is an API between the natural and spirit world.*

The above definition of an altar will be the working definition of an altar used throughout this book. Interestingly enough, if you examine any godly or ungodly altar in the Bible, they all meet these basic qualifications. It is also easy to identify the kind of altar that is functioning in someone's life by the kind of spirits, habits, or God-encounters that a person keeps experiencing. An altar of death, for instance, will cause sudden death to become a repetitive ritual in the life of its human attendants or persons controlled by it. On the other hand, an altar of supernatural favor will cause its human attendants to experience repetitive goodwill from all men regardless of race, status, or gender. We will now attempt to back up our definition of an altar with supporting Scriptures for each element of our working definition.

1. ***An altar is a supernatural landing strip.***

Genesis 28:11-12 says,

> *And he came to a certain place and stayed overnight there because the sun had set. Taking one of the stones of the place, he put it under his head and lay down there [to sleep]. [12] He dreamed that there was a ladder (stairway) placed on the earth, and the top of it reached [out of sight] toward heaven; and [he saw] the angels of God ascending and descending on it [going to and from heaven].*

When Jacob was running away from his angry brother Esau who was contemplating killing him, he came upon the same place in Bethel, where Abraham (see Genesis 12:7) had built an altar unto the LORD. This was several decades before Jacob, Abraham's grandson, was born. Jacob was arrested by God at this altar. While he slept, he dreamed that he was sleeping at the exact place, "a company of angels was ascending and descending." Why were angels ascending and descending at this physical location? Answer: there was an "altar" established by Abraham at that location. Essentially, the place Jacob chose to sleep also served as a supernatural landing strip (airport) for the angels of God. Abraham's act of worship in raising an altar at Bethel decades earlier had opened a portal for a God-encounter at this special place. It's no wonder the devil does not want God's children to establish righteous altars during their earthly pilgrimages. He is afraid that the righteous altars we raise in our generation will be used by God in the future destiny of our children and their children's children, to intercept them. It's not surprising, therefore, why Jacob called this place the gateway to heaven: *"So, he was afraid and said, 'How fearful and awesome is this place! This is none other than the house of God, and this is the gateway to heaven.'" (Genesis 28:17)*

Wherever there is a righteous altar, that place is also "the gateway to heaven!" This why Satan is afraid of righteous altars because they connect heaven and earth seamlessly.

2. *An altar is a spiritual power station.*

In 1 Kings 18:24, the prophet Elijah declares, "Then you call on the name of your god, and I will call on the name of the Lord; and the god who answers by fire, He is God." And all the people answered, "It is well spoken." In an attempt to return a spiritually backslidden nation to God, Elijah challenged the prophets of Baal, who sat at Jezebel's table to a spiritual dual on Mount Carmel before the people of Israel. He challenged the 450 prophets of Baal to build an altar to Baal and call on his name until he "powered" (fired up) the altar without using natural means of creating a fire. Why would Elijah make such an unusual request? It's because he knew that an altar is the spiritual power station of the spirit world. Since altars function as spiritual power stations, it explains why some deliverance sessions are not very effective in setting people free. They have the effect of removing light bulbs from a house without disconnecting the house from the electric grid that powers the light bulbs. Destroying an evil altar that generates demonic activity in a nation or person's life is more efficacious than merely casting out demons. Just like natural power stations can fire up appliances connected to them, so can an altar, whether it's righteous or evil. When Elijah initiated the battle of altars on Mount Carmel by issuing his unusual challenge, the people of Israel quickly answered, "It is well spoken." Since God was determined to turn the hearts of His people back to Himself, He made it impossible for the prophets of Baal to generate the 'spiritual power' they needed to affect the result they sought.

After hours of abject failure to call down fire from heaven by the prophets of Baal, Elijah, the prophet, finally admonished the people of Israel to come closer to him. It says in 1 Kings 18:30-32, *"Then Elijah said to all the people, "Come near to me." So, all the people approached him. And he repaired and rebuilt the [old] altar of the Lord that had been torn down [by Jezebel]. Then Elijah took twelve stones in accordance with the number of the tribes of the sons of Jacob, to whom the word of the Lord had come, saying, "Israel shall be your name." So, with the stones Elijah built an altar in the name of the Lord."* The Bible tells us that Elijah repaired the broken altar of the Lord, with 12 stones, according to the 12 tribes of Israel. To fully demonstrate to the people that the altar of the Lord is a supernatural power station, Elijah told the people to soak the altar he had built with plenty of water, making it impossible to start a natural fire.

An altar is a supernatural landing strip, a power station, a consecrated place, a place of exchange, a place of sacrifice, a table of fellowship, a place where covenants are made and sustained; it's a spiritual platform where spirits (God, angels or demons) land;
it is where humanity meets with divinity!

However, when Elijah called on the name of the Lord, this is what happened according to 1 Kings 18:36-39:

At the time of the offering of the evening sacrifice, Elijah the prophet approached [the altar] and said, "O Lord, the God of Abraham, Isaac, and Israel (Jacob), let it be known today that You are God in Israel and that I am Your servant and that I have done all these things at Your word. Answer me, O Lord, answer me, so that this people may know that You, O Lord, are God, and that You have turned their hearts back [to You]." Then the fire of the Lord fell and consumed the burnt offering and the wood, and even the stones and the dust; it also licked up the water in the trench. When all the people saw it, they fell face downward; and they said, "The Lord, He is God! The Lord, He is God!

Supernatural fire fell from heaven and consumed both the sacrifice and all the water on and around the altar, proving that an altar is a spiritual power station. That explains why every powerful person on earth, whether they know it or not, is standing on an altar. **No one can have real power on earth without standing on an altar!**

3. *An altar is a consecrated place.*

God is a God of consecration and requires that those who attend to His altar be consecrated for service. According to dictionary.com, the word "consecrate" literally means "to make or declare sacred; set apart or dedicate to the service of a deity." It's very clear from the meaning of the word what God requires from His human attendants to His altar. Unlike human attendants to the altars of demon-gods, where consecration is not needed, God requires it of His people. This is why all the rooms in your house should not be equal in importance. There ought to be a room (no matter how small) that is more "sacred" than any other room. When you are in this room, you behave differently from any other room.

Listen to what God says to the children of Israel about this issue in Exodus 29:43-44, *"There I will meet with the Israelites, and the Tent of Meeting shall be sanctified by My glory [the Shekinah, God's dwelling presence]. I will sanctify the Tent of Meeting and the altar [of burnt offering]; also I will sanctify Aaron and his sons to serve as priests to Me."* It's very clear from the passage that God expects not only His altar to be consecrated but also for the human attendants to the altar to follow suit. That is why God judges sin harshly in those who come near to Him! He is a holy God, so He expects His servants who attend to His altar to be holy, sanctified, and set apart, hating even garments spotted by the flesh.

4. *An altar is a place of exchange.*

Peter, the apostle, makes it clear in 1 Peter 2:24, which says,

> *He personally carried our sins in His body on the cross [willingly offering Himself on it, as on an altar of sacrifice], so that we might die to sin [becoming immune from the penalty and power of sin] and live for righteousness; for by His wounds you [who believe] have been healed.*

This verse demonstrates that the cross where Messiah Jesus was crucified became more than an instrument of torture invented by the Roman Empire. In His foreknowledge and eternal genius, God transformed it into a living altar that would deliver millions of people from the ravaging power of sin. Like any functional altar, the cross became a place of divine exchange. Saint Peter makes it clear that at the Cross, we exchanged our sins for His righteousness and our sicknesses for the stripes on His back. Since all altars are places of exchange, the cross of Christ is, without question, the most important altar ever established on earth. Over 2000 years since the crucifixion of Jesus, the cross has not lost its redemptive power as sinners and saints look to the One who shed His blood on it!

5. *An altar is a place where covenants are made and sustained.*

God is a God of covenant. It suffices to say that God cannot use a man or woman who has no covenant (agreement) with Him. However, covenants always require platforms where they can be made. Can I submit to you that the only spiritual platform that can host and sustain a covenant with God is an altar? So, to bring Abraham into a place of covenant, the Lord tested Abraham's loyalty and commitment by asking him to sacrifice his only son Isaac on an altar on Mount Moriah. When Abraham and Isaac arrived at the place on the mountain that the Lord had shown him, Abraham built an altar to the Lord. He proceeded to bind his son with rope and place him on the newly erected altar. As soon as God saw that Abraham was serious about following through, God spoke in an audible voice of heaven and admonished Abraham not to kill his son Isaac.

In response to Abraham's act of total obedience and faith, God proceeded to cut a covenant with him at the same altar he had just erected to the Lord. Here is what God said to Abraham in Genesis 22:15-18:

> *The Angel of the Lord called to Abraham from heaven a second time and said, "By Myself (on the basis of Who I Am) I have sworn [an oath], declares the Lord, that since you have done this thing and have not withheld [from Me] your son, your only son [of promise], indeed I will greatly bless you, and I will greatly multiply your descendants like the stars of the heavens and like the sand on the seashore; and your seed shall possess the gate of their enemies [as conquerors]. Through your seed all the nations of the earth shall be blessed, because you have heard and obeyed My voice.*

This passage proves that all covenants are made and sustained by altars. That is why any demonic covenants made by your forefathers (ancestors) are being maintained in your bloodline by evil altars they erected. Unless these evil altars are destroyed, the covenants (agreements) connected to them will continue to influence your life, even if you are a born-again believer in Jesus Christ.

6. ***An altar is a spiritual platform where spirits (God, angels, or demons) land.***

We live in two parallel universes, the spirit world versus the natural world of matter. For celestial beings to enter our physical world, they require a spiritual platform, an interface so-to-speak where they (spirits) can legally land or touch down on earth. This spiritual platform is what the Scriptures call an altar. So, it's not surprising that Zechariah was standing by the altar of incense when the angel Gabriel appeared to him to announce the birth of John the Baptist. It says in Luke 1:11, *"And an angel of the Lord appeared to him, standing to the right of the altar of incense."* There are no meaningless details in Scripture. The Holy Spirit went to great lengths to unmask where Zechariah was standing when the angel Gabriel showed up. He was standing next to the altar of incense. The altar was the most logical and legal choice of entry for the angel of the Lord.

7. ***An altar is where humanity meets with divinity!***

The place where divinity meets humanity is one of the most critical aspects of an altar. What can be more important in this world than hosting God and His holy angels in our lives? Absolutely nothing!

A study of the Bible from Genesis to Revelation shows us that God's favorite place for meeting with men is at an altar. In Genesis 12:7, the Bible says, *"Then the Lord appeared to Abram and said, 'I will give this land to your descendants.' So, Abram built an altar there to [honor] the Lord who had appeared to him."* As soon as Abraham built an altar unto the Lord, God wasted no time showing up at the altar visibly.

Unfortunately, since the devil also mimics God, Satan and his demonic cohorts also love to appear to people at an altar. When you build a genuine altar for the Lord, whether it's in your house, office, or your heart, get ready for God to show up.

8. *An altar is a place of sacrifice.*

We are currently living through a dispensation of time where people despise sacrifice. They want everything easy and cheap. Anything that involves both pain and sacrifice is avoided like the plague. Marriages have fallen prey to this non-sacrificing spirit, resulting in myriads of divorces. This spirit of entitlement and self-centeredness has infected many members of the body of Christ. Unfortunately for them, God's word says, *"Gather My godly ones to Me, those who have made a covenant with Me by sacrifice."* God blesses people who are able to make a covenant with Him by sacrifice. The million-dollar question is, why? It's because the Bible clearly demonstrates that all altars are fueled by sacrifice. Every altar is known by the sacrifices that are slaughtered on it. In 1 Kings 3:4, the Bible says:

> The king went to Gibeon [near Jerusalem, where the tabernacle and the bronze altar stood] to sacrifice there, for that was the great high place. Solomon offered a thousand burnt offerings on that altar. [5] In Gibeon the Lord appeared to Solomon in a dream at night; and God said, "Ask [Me] what I shall give you.

After preparing a large sacrifice and offering it on the altar to the Lord, the Lord quickly spoke to the young King Solomon. In the chapter on the 12 Laws of Altars, we will look in great detail at why all altars are fueled and powered by the sacrifices of their human attendants.

9. *An altar is a place of worship.*

There is no higher calling in the lives of all believers in Messiah Jesus than to worship God. We were created to worship God with all our heart, mind, and soul. Even on evil altars, worship is the ultimate spiritual currency that animates them. It's no wonder Jesus told the woman at the well in John 4:23-24, *"But a time is coming and is already here when the true worshipers will worship the Father in spirit [from the heart, the inner self] and in truth;*

for the Father seeks such people to be His worshipers. God is spirit [the Source of life, yet invisible to mankind], and those who worship Him must worship in spirit and truth." In Jesus' estimation, worship is what our heavenly Father seeks the most. According to the Scriptures, worshiping God requires building an altar, whether physically or spiritually, in our hearts. In Genesis 12:8, we see a physical altar that enabled Abraham to enter into a time of worship. It says, *"Then he moved on from there to the mountain on the east of Bethel, and pitched his tent, with Bethel on the west and Ai on the east; and there he built an altar to the Lord and called on the name of the Lord [in worship through prayer, praise, and thanksgiving]."*

Even on evil altars worship is the ultimate spiritual
currency that animates them.

10. *An altar is a place of prayer.*

An altar is a place of prayer! Prayer is one of the most essential activities of an altar. The late Dr. Myles Munroe interprets prayer as follows: "prayer is an earthly license for heavenly interference in the affairs of men." This definition of prayer is weighty, life-transforming, and directly connected to the subject of altars. It suggests that God requires legal permission to interfere in the affairs of men. The only platform that God can stand on to gain legal access to the world of men is on an altar. Prayer acts as a spiritual kindling to the fire that burns on the altar. That is what transpired in Luke 1:8-10 when the angel Gabriel appeared to Zechariah, as it says:

> *Now it happened while Zacharias was serving as priest before God in the appointed order of his priestly division, as was the custom of the priesthood, he was chosen by lot to enter [the sanctuary of] the temple of the Lord and burn incense [on the altar of incense]. And all the congregation was praying outside [in the court of the temple] at the hour of the incense offering.*

Any attendant to an altar who is weak in prayer is weak as a factor in the work of God. Praying continually is how a human attendant can strengthen the altar and his or her connection to it. Through the spirit of prayer, the altar flows into the attendant and the attendant into the altar. In the place of prayer, the attendant to an altar begins to become one with the altar. A prayer-less attendant to an altar weakens the power and voice of the altar.

11. *An altar is a table of fellowship.*

According to my spiritual daughter, Karen Johnson, who pastors Olive Tree Connections in Nashville, there is a practice in a Hebrew family called "Bircath Hamazon – Benshen," which is where the kitchen table is transformed into an "altar" before God. At that "altar," the family learns of fellowship, education, evangelism, instruction in Torah, and prayer. The Table (Shulchan) now becomes the altar of God. That is why true evangelism from a Hebraic mindset would be to learn at the altar (table) and bring other people to that altar (table). This tradition is seen in Acts 2:42, *"They were continually and faithfully devoting themselves to the instruction of the apostles, and to fellowship, to eating meals together and to prayers."* According to the book of Acts, they were discussing Torah around the table (altar). They broke bread together, where they enjoyed fellowship and evangelism. They had a common meal, and they entered into the ceremony called "Bircath Hamazon – Benshen."

That is why it is spiritually dangerous to prepare food in the kitchen when you are "angry" with your spouse or children. That negative energy gets into the food and defiles the altar of fellowship – not to mention the danger of eating food prepared by angry chefs at some of the restaurants we love to patronize. Some of you used to be very calm and collected, but ever since you ate the food of a person filled with rage, you now find that you have spats of anger that were not there before. That is why I pray over my food and ask the Holy Spirit to remove any demonic energies released into the food during its preparation.

12. *An altar is also a system of authorization for promises, vows, and agreements.*

Then Laban declared, 'This pile of stones will stand as a witness to remind us of the covenant we have made today.' [This explains why it was called Galeed — "Witness Pile."] But it was also called Mizpah (which means "watchtower"), for Laban said, "May the Lord keep watch between us to make sure that we keep this covenant when we are out of each other's sight. [50] If you mistreat my daughters or if you marry other wives, God will see it even if no one else does. He is a witness to this covenant between us. [51] "See this pile of stones," Laban continued, "and see this monument I have set between us. [52] They stand between us as witnesses of our vows. I will never pass this pile of stones to harm you, and you must never pass these stones or this monument to harm me. [53] I call on the God of our ancestors—the God of your grandfather Abraham and the God of my grandfather Nahor—to serve as a judge between us." So Jacob took an oath before the fearsome God of his father, Isaac, to respect the boundary line.

(Genesis 31:48-53)

Altars are also systems of authorization for promises, vows, and agreements made between man with man or man with divinity. We have such an example in Scripture concerning the vow and agreement established between Jacob and his father-in-law Laban. This took place after Laban and his troops caught up with Jacob, who had left Syria in the secrecy of the night without bidding farewell to his father-in-law. Jacob took Laban's two daughters, Leah and Rachel, as well as the children he had fathered through them and their maids.

Laban was very furious with Jacob. He was going to kill him. However, by the time he caught up to him, God already intercepted him in a dream and placed him under a divine restraining order. God told Laban not to harm Jacob; to speak to him neither good nor bad. Even though Laban complained bitterly about how Jacob had left him unceremoniously, he nevertheless settled for the covenant they made. The covenant, or agreement, contained promises and vows to which the two men were tied. Both men invited God to become a witness to the promises, vows, and agreement that the two gentlemen made with each other at an altar! They took a large stone and heaped many smaller stones on top of it and then made a covenant with each other and with God. So, this "altar" would serve as a system of authorization for the promises, vows, and agreement they had just made.

13. *An altar is an API between the natural and spirit world.*

We live in an age of human development and evolution characterized by stunning advances in both science and technology. So, I asked the Holy Spirit to show me something that we can all relate to so I could convey the concept behind an altar. The Holy Spirit did not disappoint. He said to me, "Francis, an altar in the Bible, functions in much the same way as an API in connecting different technology platforms." For those who don't know what an API is, let me allow Wikipedia to define it for you.

DEFINING API: "An application programming interface (API) is a computing interface that defines interactions between multiple software intermediaries. It defines the kinds of calls or requests that can be made, how to make them, the data formats that should be used, the conventions to follow, etc. It can also provide extension mechanisms so that users can extend existing functionality in various ways and to varying degrees. An API can be entirely custom, specific to a component, or designed based on an industry-standard to ensure interoperability. Through information hiding, APIs enable modular programming, allowing users to use the interface independently of the implementation."[1]

The Holy Spirit showed me that API's primary technology was already built into the biblical platforms known as altars. Like API in modern technological platforms, altars essentially facilitate and define the multiple interactions between spirits and humans and the engagement protocols. Like API, altars also facilitate and monitor the exchange of goods and services between divinity and humanity. Like their biblical counterparts (altars), API's function as systems of authorization within technology platforms. It's actually impossible for Bank of America to do business online with Chase Bank without going through an API (altar). In much the same way, transacting with 'divinity' is impossible without going through a spiritual API, the Scripture calls an altar!

Two Types of Altars

And in the course of time Cain brought to the Lord an offering of the fruit of the ground. ⁴ And Abel brought of the firstborn of his flock and of the fat portions. And the Lord had respect and regard for Abel and for his offering, ⁵ But for [Cain and his offering He had no respect or regard. So Cain was exceedingly angry and indignant, and he looked sad and depressed.

(Genesis 4:3-5)

In Scripture, there are two basic types of altars, namely: righteous and evil. The first time in Scripture that we are confronted with this distinction is in the fourth chapter of the book of Genesis when the two sons of Adam, Cain, and Abel decided to build altars to offer their sacrificial offerings to the Lord. According to Scripture, Cain brought the Lord an offering of the fruit of the ground. Cain, who was an agricultural farmer, placed vegetables on his altar. On the other hand, Abel brought of the firstborn of his flock and of the fat portions. God's reaction to the offerings on the two altars was pretty telling.

God demonstrably rejected Cain's offering, while He demonstrably accepted and showered with favor Abel's sacrificial offering. Why did God reject Cain's offering? Because God had already cursed the ground in Genesis 3:17, *"And to Adam He said, Because you have listened and given heed to the voice of your wife and have eaten of the tree of which I commanded you, saying, You shall not eat of it, the ground is under a curse because of you; in sorrow and toil shall you eat [of the fruits] of it all the days of your life."* How can God use the fruit of the "accursed" to redeem the soul of man? That is why He had no pleasure in Cain's offering. I am certain Adam had already told his two sons that the Lord had cursed the ground because of his sin. So why would

Cain bring an offering from something that was already cursed? How could he secure atonement for his soul using such a thing?

Why did he do it? I believe he was driven by rebellion, pride, and the desire to do his own thing. God's rejection of Cain's offering shows us that He is very selective of what's given to Him at a righteous altar. This separates God from idols (demon-gods) who will accept any accursed thing offered to them by their human attendants. Idols are so desperate for expression in the world of men that they will accept any offering, provided they can gain access to mankind. On the other hand, God is sovereign, holy, and separate from sinners, so He cannot be manipulated by the human attendants to His altar. He accepted Abel's offering because Abel gave Him precisely what He required for the remission of sins – the blood of an innocent animal, from the best of his flock!

Consequentially, Cain became the biblical symbol for an evil and defiled altar. His altar was built on evil, pride, defiance, rebellion, rage, jealousy, selfish ambition, and murder. The god behind Cain's evil altar was the "idol of self" and, ultimately, Satan. This is why Cain could resist and argue with God. Look at this: *"And the Lord said to Cain, 'Where is Abel your brother?' And he said, 'I do not know. Am I my brother's keeper?"* Look at the arrogance in Cain's answer. Who talks to God with such disrespect, pride, and arrogance? Every person who is an attendant to an evil altar built for the idol in their life. That may explain why some Christ-professing Christians are so full of pride and arrogance – their hearts are full of idols and evil altars!

Two Dimensions of Altars: Stationery & Mobile

> *Then Elijah took twelve stones in accordance with the number of the tribes of the sons of Jacob, to whom the word of the Lord had come, saying, "Israel shall be your name." [32] So with the stones Elijah built an altar in the name of the Lord.*
>
> *(1 Kings 18:31-32)*

STATIONARY ALTARS

Whereas there are two types of altars – righteous and evil – there are nevertheless two spiritual "dimensions" of altars mentioned in Scripture, namely, stationary or mobile. By definition, a stationary altar is unmovable and always restricted to a particular geographical location. Most of the altars in the Old Testament fall under this category. For instance, the altar that God used at Bethel to intercept Jacob when he was running away from Esau was a stationary altar. God couldn't touch him until he arrived at the geographical location where the altar was. Also, a family altar is an example of a stationary altar within the home where the family can meet as a unit to have devotions and meet with God. Unfortunately, the devil has destroyed many family altars. That's why we have so many broken families.

Jesus was sitting next to a stationary altar in the temple when He noticed that the widow gave her last, in contrast to the rich Pharisees who gave God little in comparison to how much they had in their possession.

> *And He sat down opposite the [temple] treasury and began watching how the people were putting money into the treasury. And many rich people were putting in large sums. ⁴²A poor widow came and put in two small copper coins, which amount to a mite. ⁴³Calling His disciples to Him, He said to them, "I assure you and most solemnly say to you, this poor widow put in [proportionally] more than all the contributors to the treasury. ⁴⁴For they all contributed from their surplus, but she, from her poverty, put in all she had, all she had to live on.*
>
> *(Mark 12:41-44).*

Since receiving the revelation on altars, I have dedicated one room, or space in every house where I have lived, to consecrate an altar to the Lord. Some of the most powerful supernatural encounters I have ever had happened when I spent time with the Lord inside my personal altar.

The Sin of Transgressing a Stationery Altar

So, if you are presenting your offering at the altar, and while there you remember that your brother has something [such as a grievance or legitimate complaint] against you, 24 leave your offering there at the altar and go. First make peace with your brother, and then come and present your offering. 25 Come to terms quickly [at the earliest opportunity] with your opponent at law while you are with him on the way [to court], so that your opponent does not hand you over to the judge, and the judge to the guard, and you are thrown into prison.

(Matthew 5:23-25)

The above passage of Scripture from the Gospel of Matthew is very telling indeed. What is scary about it is that the warning came directly from the mouth of the Lord Jesus Christ. If anyone on earth knew and understood the critical importance of altars in the economy of God, it was the Lord Jesus Christ, the incarnate Son of God! Jesus, in the above passage, offers us a stern warning that we would do well to heed. Jesus addresses an issue that happens in churches all the time. Unfortunately, this is because of a lack of teaching on the subject of altars and their sacredness to God. In the above passage of Scripture, the Lord Jesus says, *"If you are presenting your offering at the altar, and while there you remember that your brother has something [such as a grievance or legitimate complaint] against you, leave your offering there at the altar and go. First, make peace with your brother, and then come and present your offering."*

I want you to prayerfully meditate on the implications of what Jesus is saying here. How many Christians are angry and unforgiving of their brothers and sisters in the Lord? And yet Sunday after Sunday, they come to the altar of the Lord at their local place of worship and give an offering to Him, all the while harboring unforgiveness toward their brothers and sisters.

As the senior pastor of my church, I sadly have to report that the above scenario happens a lot. Could this be the explanation behind why so many Christians are languishing in frustration because their destinies and the things

God promised them seemed to be in a holding pattern no matter how much they fast and pray? Listen to Jesus describe the far-reaching spiritual consequences of transgressing a stationary altar such as a consecrated pulpit in a local church. In Matthew 5:25-26, Jesus describes the punishment for transgressing a consecrated stationery altar this way, *"Come to terms quickly [at the earliest opportunity] with your opponent at law while you are with him on the way [to court], so that your opponent does not hand you over to the judge, and the judge to the guard, and you are thrown into prison. I assure you and most solemnly say to you, you will not come out of there until you have paid the last cent."* The Holy Spirit showed me that many Christians are actually in a spiritual prison in the spirit world for violating Jesus' admonition concerning the proper treatment of the altar of the Lord in His temple. That is why they are in endless cycles of drama and pain. If the shoe fits, please stop here and repent! God will set you free and parole you from your spiritual jail cell.

MOBILE ALTARS

Suddenly the Lord said to Moses, Aaron, and Miriam, "Come out, you three, to the Tent of Meeting (tabernacle)." And the three of them came out. [5] The Lord came down in a pillar of cloud and stood at the doorway of the tabernacle, and He called Aaron and Miriam, and they came forward. [6] And He said, "Hear now My words: If there is a prophet among you, I the Lord will make Myself known to him in a vision and I will speak to him in a dream. [7] "But it is not so with My servant Moses; He is entrusted and faithful in all My house. [8] "With him I speak mouth to mouth [directly], Clearly and openly and not in riddles; and he beholds the form of the Lord. Why then were you not afraid to speak against My servant Moses?"

(Numbers 12:4-8)

We live in a world where science and technology are changing the way we interact and do business in ways that were considered impossible just two decades ago. Those of you who are older may remember when all phones were landlines hardwired to the wall. If you happened to be outside when the phone rang, you had to run inside the house to answer the phone. God help you if your car broke down on the road. You had to catch a ride or wait for the police to have access to a phone. What a nightmare this must have been! We can only imagine. Fortunately, mobile phone technology changed all of that! Today, we carry our phones in our hands and answer them with the touch of a finger. Without a doubt, mobile phone technology supersedes the old technology of stationary phones. That said, stationery phone technology is very useful for carrying out business in corporate offices and government institutions where cell phone use is prohibited.

Similarly, mobile altars are more efficient and supersede stationery altars because they are more dynamic and can cover a wide range by virtue of their mobility. In the first chapter of this book, I mentioned that when God encounters a man He wants to use to change a generation, an altar is born. This altar is mobile because it is the man or woman God chooses who becomes a meeting place for divinity and humanity. It is the man (e.g., Benny Hinn) or woman (e.g., Kathryn Khulman) God chooses to use who becomes a supernatural landing strip for God and His holy angels to influence the destiny of nations. That is why God was very upset with Aaron and Miriam for contending with Moses over his choice of a wife. It was none of their business!

In God's eyes, Moses was very sacred to Him because the man Moses, as of the third chapter of Exodus, had become a consecrated mobile altar for God encounters. That is why Egypt was rocked with miracles, signs, and wonders wherever Moses went! Here is how the Bible summarizes the life of Moses in Deuteronomy 34:10-12, *"Since that time no prophet has risen in Israel like Moses, whom the Lord knew face to face, [11] [none equal to him] in all the signs and wonders which the Lord sent him to perform in the land of Egypt against Pharaoh, all his servants, and all his land, [12] and in all the mighty power and all the great and terrible deeds which Moses performed in the sight of all Israel."*

The Sin of Transgressing a Mobile Altar

And the anger of the Lord was kindled against Miriam and Aaron, and He departed. [10] But when the cloud had withdrawn from over the tent, behold,

Miriam was leprous, as white as snow. And Aaron turned and looked at Miriam, and, behold, she was leprous.

(Numbers 12:9)

As soon as Moses finished speaking all these words, the ground under them split open; ³² and the earth opened its mouth and swallowed them and their households, and all the men who supported Korah, with all their possessions. ³³ So they and all that belonged to them went down alive to Sheol; and the earth closed over them, and they perished from among the assembly. ³⁴ All Israel who were around them fled at their outcry, for they said, "The earth may swallow us also." ³⁵ Fire also came forth from the Lord and consumed the two hundred and fifty men who were offering the incense.

(Numbers 16:31-35)

God was very angry with the sin of Aaron and Miriam. What was their sin? They committed a transgression by foolishly opposing a mobile altar – Moses! Before the Holy Spirit gave me the revelation on the strategic importance of altars in the economy of God, I was like most mercy-minded Christians. I thought God was pretty harsh with some of the transgressions of the people of the old covenant. I was taken aback when I saw how God caused the earth to swallow thousands of people who turned against Moses in a rebellion spearheaded by the sons of Korah. But all my foolish thoughts and humanistic thinking dissolved once the Holy Spirit told me, "Francis, God was not protecting a man. He was protecting a mobile altar, a consecrated and surrendered one at that!" I was stunned speechless, but my spirit was filled with joy. I realized how far God was willing to go to preserve a mobile altar located in a man or woman who was fully surrendered to His Spirit. It inspired me to become such an altar to my generation.

Many of you reading this book, your lives are in a holding pattern because Satan tempted you to foolishly challenge a consecrated mobile altar for God's Kingdom at one point in your spiritual journey. Like the conniving serpent he is, Satan then ran into the Courts of Heaven with evidence of your transgression and asked the Righteous Judge for permission to hold your destiny in a holding pattern until the day you repent! Just remember Satan is a master double dealer! You are foolish to trust anything he tells you to do, especially against the Lord's anointed. David knew this. That is why he was never tempted to kill King Saul with his own hands. He did not want the blood of the Lord's anointed on his hands!

ɷɷɷ

When we allow idols, which are essentially demons, to build altars in our souls, these demon-gods become the guiding spirits in our lives.

ɷɷɷ

The Sin of Worshipping at an Evil Altar

> *Then all the people of the land went to the house of Baal and tore it down. They utterly smashed his altar and his images to pieces, and they put Mattan the priest of Baal to death in front of the altars. And [Jehoiada] the priest appointed officers over the house of the Lord.*
>
> *(2 Kings 11:18)*

I've already shown you that sins against the altar of God are treated very seriously by the Holy Spirit. So, in God's eyes, there is no sin against the altar that is more egregious to Him than to have a human being He created worshiping idols and serving at an evil altar dedicated to Satan and his demonic kingdom. In the above passage of Scripture, when the spirit of revival came upon the children of Israel, everyone rose and went to the house of Baal and tore it down. And while they were at it, they completely smashed Baal's altar and every image connected to the worship of Baal. Suddenly they turned on Mattan, the priest of Baal, and put him to death in front of these evil altars. Hell is full of humans burning in unquenchable flames of fire because during their earthly pilgrimage; they chose to worship the creature (Satan) more than the Creator, who is blessed forevermore! The judgment of the Mattan's of this present age is written fearfully in Romans 1:24-25:

> *Therefore God gave them over in the lusts of their own hearts to [sexual] impurity, so that their bodies would be dishonored among them [abandoning them to the degrading power of sin], 25 because [by choice] they exchanged the truth of God for a lie, and worshiped and served the creature rather than the Creator, who is blessed forever! Amen.*

∽∽∽∽∽

There is no sin against the altar that is more egregious to Him than to have a human being He created worshiping idols and serving at an evil altar that is dedicated to Satan and his demonic kingdom.

∽∽∽∽∽

PRAYER OF ACTIVATION!

"Heavenly Father, I ask for the Court of Heaven to be seated and for the books of my destiny to be opened as I come before the Judge of all the earth to plead my case against any evil altar in my life or bloodline that is speaking against me. I decree and declare that the Holy Spirit is my official guide and counselor in this courtroom. Heavenly Father, I surrender all rights to self-representation; instead, I ask my defense attorney and mediator of the new covenant, the Lord Jesus Christ, to represent me in your Royal Courtroom against all idols and evil altars that are controlling my life and bloodline, in any way. I also ask the Lord Jesus to heal me by His blood from all soul wounds caused by idols and evil altars in my bloodline. I am seeking a verdict of release from the power of these evil altars, in Jesus' name.

I now enter a plea of 'guilty' into the court's records concerning any legitimate accusations that Satan has filed in Court against me or my bloodline. For Jesus said, in Matthew 5:25, *"Come to terms quickly [at the earliest opportunity] with your opponent at law while you are with him on the way [to court], so that your opponent does not hand you over to the judge, and the judge to the guard, and you are thrown into prison."* Lord, since I am under oath, I cannot lie about my sinful activities and the iniquities of my bloodline that are connected to idolatry and the erecting evil altars. I repent for all sins and transgressions that I and my ancestors ever committed against you and the laws of nature. Cleanse me from all sin by the blood of Jesus, according to 1 John 1:9. I now formally submit my guilty plea and repentance to the court, in Jesus' Name."

Heavenly Father,

- I decree and declare that every evil altar speaking against me is completely destroyed, in Jesus' Name.
- I decree and declare that every evil altar acting as an evil supernatural landing strip against me is completely destroyed, in Jesus' Name.
- I decree and declare that every evil altar acting as an evil supernatural power station against me is completely destroyed in Jesus' Name.
- I decree and declare that every evil altar ever consecrated to Satan by any of my ancestors is completely destroyed in Jesus' Name.
- I decree and declare that I give back everything Satan gave my ancestors in exchange for erecting evil altars in our bloodline, in Jesus' Name.
- I decree and declare that every covenant my ancestors cut with evil altars is completely destroyed, in Jesus' Name.
- I decree and declare that every sacrifice or offering my ancestors gave to evil altars will no longer influence my life, in Jesus' Name.
- I decree and declare that I am a mobile altar God can use to win souls and advance His Kingdom in the Earth, in Jesus' Name.

LIFE APPLICATION

Memory Verse

"Now it happened while Zacharias was serving as priest before God in the appointed order of his priestly division, as was the custom of the priesthood, he was chosen by lot to enter [the sanctuary of] the temple of the Lord and burn incense [on the altar of incense]. And all the congregation was praying outside [in the court of the temple] at the hour of the incense offering."

Luke 1:8-10

Reflections

1. Explain this statement; an altar is a place of exchange?

_____

_____

_____

_____

2. Explain this statement; an altar is a spiritual landing strip?

_____

_____

_____

_____

4

Godly & Evil Altars

Then God said, "Let Us make man in Our image, according to Our likeness;
let them have dominion over the fish of the sea, over the birds of the air, and
over the cattle, over all the earth and over every creeping thing that creeps on
the earth.

(Genesis 1:26)

In the previous chapter on the Law of Dominion, we talked about its spiritual implications. We made it clear the Law of Dominion, or the Law of Territory, makes it impossible for God and celestial beings to operate on this planet we call Earth without requiring the permission of a human being. This essentially means that both God and His angels and the devil and his demon spirits need permission from a human to operate legally in the earth realm. Consequently, the Law of Dominion created a dire need for an agreed-upon or dedicated landing strip that the Bible refers to as an altar. This chapter will highlight the spiritual dynamics of altars and how they operate to either enthrone God or demon-gods. Understanding the Law of Dominion will prevent you from falling into the trap so many Christians fall into by thinking that the subject of altars is Old Testament teaching. Nothing can be further from the truth than relegating the sacred subject of altars to the Old Testament.

The subject of altars in the Bible begins in heaven itself at the altar of Melchizedek, where the Heavenly Father made Yeshua (God the Word) the "lamb slain" before the foundation of the world. Revelation 13:8, which says, *"And all the inhabitants of the earth will fall down in adoration and pay him homage, everyone whose name has not been recorded in the Book of Life of the Lamb that was slain [in sacrifice] from the foundation of the world."* The subject and spiritual technology of altars came to earth when two of Adam's sons, Cain and Abel, built two separate altars to sacrifice to the Lord. The subject of altars is picked up again in the Gospels by Jesus Himself and climaxes on the highest altar ever established on earth – the Cross upon which Messiah gave His life at a place known as Golgotha (the place of the skull)! In this book, an entire chapter is dedicated to demonstrate how God transformed an instrument of torture and punishment, such as the cross, into the highest living and righteous altar on earth!

Godly Altars

This chapter will give you a prophetic commentary on the subject of godly and evil altars. Most importantly, I want to use this chapter to demonstrate that we cannot overthrow the power of idols (demon-gods) in our lives if we fail to address the evil altars built to these idols in our generational bloodline or the unhealed areas of our soul!

The Bible is full of examples of godly and righteous altars that were raised or elected by godly men and women who loved God and served their generation with the purpose for which God created them. We will take a quick bird's eye view of these righteous altars and the men who raised them. The names of altars are derived from observing the deity that is worshiped and the perpetual activity that transpires around the altar.

I. NOAH'S ALTAR

And Noah built an altar to the Lord, and took of every [ceremonially] clean animal and of every clean bird and offered burnt offerings on the altar. ²¹ The Lord smelled the pleasing aroma [a soothing, satisfying scent] and the Lord said to Himself, "I will never again curse the ground because of man, for the intent (strong inclination, desire) of man's heart is wicked from his youth; and I will never again destroy every living thing, as I have done.

(Genesis 8:20-21)

The first thing that Noah did when he came out of the ark was to build God an altar. The Bible goes into great detail about the first altar established by man after the destruction of the entire human race by the flood. This altar of Noah would signify a new beginning between God and man. Noah went to great lengths to ensure that the sacrificial offering he placed on this altar to the Lord was based upon very clean birds and animals. The Bible says the Lord smelled the pleasing aroma that came from Noah's altar. Altars speak whether they are righteous or evil altars.

It seems Noah's altar spoke loudly, clearly, and beautifully. God's reaction to the altar seems to suggest that this altar became the one that reverses curses. Noah's altar caused God to begin to speak to Himself about never cursing the ground or destroying the entire human population through a global flood. It's interesting to note that there has never been a global flood capable of drowning the entire world ever since then. Needless to say, God has kept the promise He made after He was touched by Noah's altar. So, Noah's altar shows us that there are righteous altars that "break and reverse curses!"

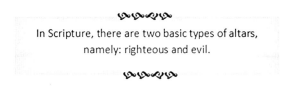

In Scripture, there are two basic types of altars, namely: righteous and evil.

II. ABRAHAM'S ALTAR

Then the Lord appeared to Abram and said, "I will give this land to your descendants." So, Abram built an altar there to [honor] the Lord who had appeared to him. ⁸ Then he moved on from there to the mountain on the east of Bethel, and pitched his tent, with Bethel on the west and Ai on the east; and there he built an altar to the Lord and called on the name of the Lord[in worship through prayer, praise, and thanksgiving].

(Genesis 12:7-8)

The first thing that Abraham did when he arrived in the Promised land was to build an altar to the Lord, who had called him from Ur of the Chaldeans. Before he marked his territory in the land, he made sure to secure his inheritance by raising an altar. Raising an altar was Abraham's way of possessing the land God had promised him and his descendants. This exposes us to a very powerful principle for marking and possessing territory, in the natural and the spirit. We need to raise an altar to speak for us over the land and overthrow the evil altars that are also staking their claim over the land or piece of property God wants to give us! The Lord appeared to Abraham immediately at the altar he had just raised, proving that altars are places of meetings or divine encounters with God. It would seem that the name of the altar that Abraham erected to the Lord is an "altar that gathers or an altar of possession." Today the land of Palestine, or Canaan, currently belongs to the children of Israel just as God had promised Abraham generations earlier.

III. THE ALTAR AT MOUNT MORIAH

When they came to the place of which God had told him, Abraham built an altar there and arranged the wood, and bound Isaac his son and placed him on the altar, on top of the wood. ¹⁰ Abraham reached out his hand and took the knife to kill his son. ¹¹ But the Angel of the Lord called to him from heaven and said, "Abraham, Abraham!" He answered, "Here I am." ¹² The Lord said, "Do not reach out [with the knife in] your hand against the boy, and do nothing to [harm] him; for now I know that you fear God [with reverence and profound respect], since you have not withheld from Me your son, your only son [of promise]." ¹³ Then Abraham looked up and glanced around, and behold, behind him was a ram caught in a thicket by his horns. And Abraham went and took the ram and offered it up for a burnt offering (ascending sacrifice) instead of his son. ¹⁴ So Abraham named that place The Lord Will Provide. And it is said to this day, "On the mountain of the Lord it will be seen and provided." ¹⁵ The Angel of the Lord called to Abraham from heaven a second time ¹⁶ and said, "By Myself (on the basis of Who I Am) I have sworn [an oath], declares the Lord, that since you have done this thing and have not withheld [from Me] your son, your only son [of promise], ¹⁷ indeed I will greatly bless you, and I will greatly multiply your descendants like the stars of the heavens and like the sand on the seashore; and your seed shall possess the gate of their enemies [as conquerors]

(Genesis 22:9-17)

The second and the most critical altar that Father Abraham erected to God was the altar at Mount Moriah. One day, after Isaac's birth, the long-awaited and promised son, the Lord tested Abraham's commitment to God. God told him to go to Mount Moriah and build an altar there. He was to sacrifice his only son Isaac! Abraham did not even hesitate, even though this was a very difficult decision to make. The decision was so difficult that Abraham did not tell Sarah where he was going or his actual intentions for taking Isaac with him. I believe had Sarah known what Abraham was up to, she would have killed him before allowing him to sacrifice her only son. She knew that the living God who had revealed Himself to them was unlike the Gentile gods because He did not believe in human sacrifice.

Abraham took Isaac and some servants, and they went on the long journey to Mount Moriah. When they arrived, Abraham left his servants at the mountain base while he and Isaac climbed to the top. At the top, they began to build an altar to the Lord. Isaac, in a moment of candor, asked his father this question, "Father, I see the wood, but where is the sacrifice we are going to place on the altar?" Abraham probably failed to look him in the eye but answered confidently: "My son, God will provide for Himself a lamb!" Most likely, he then bound Isaac and placed him on the altar.

Abraham raised his knife to kill his son when suddenly, there came a voice from heaven. It was the voice of the Angel of the Lord. The Angel of the Lord told Abraham that he was not to kill his son. The Lord was only testing him, and now the Lord knew that Abraham truly feared God because he did not withhold his only son from God's righteous demand. God showed him a ram caught in the thicket right behind him that he could use to sacrifice in the place of his son Isaac. Immediately after this, the Angel of the Lord spoke to Abram from heaven a second time and made a vow to flood Abraham's life, and that of his descendants, with the miracle of total provision. It would seem the altar at Mount Moriah that Abraham built was an "altar of total obedience as well as total provision!" It is no wonder the Jewish people are blessed financially and technologically all over the world. I believe it's because God is still reacting to Abraham's obedience at Mount Moriah. Such is the power of a righteous altar!

IV. JACOB'S ALTAR

Then God said to Jacob, "Go up to Bethel and live there, and make an altar there to God, who appeared to you [in a distinct manifestation] when you fled [years ago] from Esau your brother." [2] Then Jacob said to his household and to all who were with him, "Get rid of the [idols and images of] foreign gods that are among you, and ceremonially purify yourselves and change [into fresh] clothes; [3]then let us get up and go up to Bethel, and I will make an altar there to God, who answered me in the day of my distress and has been with me wherever I have gone." [4] So they gave Jacob all the [idols and images of the] foreign gods they had and the rings which were in their ears [worn as charms against evil], and Jacob buried them under the oak tree near Shechem. [5]As they journeyed, there was a great [supernatural] terror [sent from God] on the cities around them, and [for that reason] the Canaanites did not pursue

the sons of Jacob. 6 So Jacob came to Luz (that is, Bethel), which is in the land
of Canaan, he and all the people who were with him.

(Genesis 35:1-6)

One of the first things that Jacob did, as he was heading back to the promised land after spending three decades in the land of Syria with his father-in-law Laban, was to build an altar. Jacob was concerned that the neighboring gentile nations through whose lands they were traveling would attack him to pillage his many possessions and even rape the women. This thought bothered him much, so he turned to the Lord for counsel, and the Lord told him to go back to the altar at Bethel, where he had first encountered God (see Genesis 28:11-14).

However, God had some very stringent conditions that He wanted met before He could allow Jacob to raise Him an altar that had spiritual stature and a voice in the Courts of Heaven. God told him to get rid of the idols and images of foreign gods among his children and servants. When Jacob and his children obeyed the Lord, God sent a great and supernatural terror or fear of Jacob into the hearts of these Gentile nations. So, the Canaanites did not attempt to attack Jacob and his sons. They traveled to the promised land, safely. The Bible says God's response to Jacob's altar was so powerful that the inhabitants of the land felt like it was a troop of thousands following Jacob. They were terrified and never bothered him. It appears the name of this altar at Bethel. that both Abraham and Jacob had raised to God. was an altar of supernatural protection, proving that one of the quickest ways to guarantee our safety in dangerous environments is to raise a powerful and righteous altar to the Lord.

V.   GIDEON'S ALTAR

Then the Angel of the Lord put out the end of the staff that was in His hand
and touched the meat and the unleavened bread; and fire flared up from the
rock and consumed the meat and the unleavened bread. Then the Angel of the
Lord vanished from his sight. ²²When Gideon realized [without any doubt]
that He was the Angel of the Lord, he declared, "Oh no, Lord God! For now

I have seen the Angel of the Lord face to face [and I am doomed]!" [23]*The Lord said to him, "Peace to you, do not be afraid; you shall not die."* [24]*Then Gideon built an altar there to the Lord and named it The Lord is Peace. To this day it is still in Ophrah, of the Abiezrites.*

(Judges 6:21-24)

One of my most favorite judges in the Bible is Gideon. His story about altars fascinates me. It proves to me that anyone who takes the subject of altars seriously can completely change their life. When the Angel of the Lord appeared to Gideon, the Bible said he was threshing wheat in a winepress, which is not the best place for threshing wheat. He was threshing wheat in the winepress because he was afraid of the Midianites. At the time, the Lord had delivered the children of Israel into the hands of the Midianites because the Israelites had chosen to worship the gods of the Midianites instead of the living God who brought them out of Egypt.

So, when the Angel of God arrived, there was no one more surprised than Gideon. However, Gideon was not fully aware that he was talking to God Most High until the Angel of the Lord put out the end of his staff and touched the meat and unleavened bread that he had prepared. That's when Gideon discovered, to his great dismay, that he had seen God face-to-face! He was terrified because he thought he was going to die. Instead, the Lord said to him, "Peace to you, do not be afraid; you shall not die." In worshipful response, Gideon built an altar to the Lord. Gideon called the altar the "Lord is peace!" It was not long before God commanded Gideon, who was standing on this altar of peace, to go and destroy the evil altar of Baal of his father's house. This act would lead to an explosive breakthrough in his leadership skills and destiny. It also established him as one of the most powerful judges in Israel. He completely delivered the children of Israel from the Midianites and plundered their wealth.

VI. SAMUEL'S ALTAR

So, Samuel took a nursing lamb and offered it as a whole burnt offering to the Lord; and Samuel cried out to the Lord for Israel and the Lord answered him.

¹⁰As Samuel was offering up the burnt offering, the Philistines approached for the battle against Israel. Then the Lord thundered with a great voice that day against the Philistines and threw them into confusion, and they were defeated and fled before Israel. ¹¹And the men of Israel came out of Mizpah and pursued the Philistines, and struck them down as far as [the territory] below Beth-car. ¹²Then Samuel took a stone and set it between Mizpah and Shen, and he named it Ebenezer (stone of help), saying, "Thus far the Lord has helped us." ¹³So the Philistines were subdued and they did not come anymore into Israelite territory. And the hand of the Lord was against the Philistines all the days of Samuel. ¹⁴The cities which the Philistines had taken from Israel were restored to Israel, from Ekron to Gath; and Israel recovered the cities' territory from the Philistines. Also, there was peace between Israel and the Amorites.

(1 Samuel 7:9-14)

One of my most favorite prophetic voices in the Old Testament is the Prophet Samuel. Especially since the Lord Himself once told me that my life would be like unto the prophet Samuel. He told me that the word that comes out of my mouth would not fall to the ground unfulfilled. Very humbling! One day there came a time when the Philistines were about to attack the children of Israel, and the people of God were terrified! So, they cried to the Prophet Samuel to talk to the Lord on their behalf. However, the first thing the Prophet Samuel did was ask them to get rid of all the idols and images of foreign gods that they were hiding in their houses.

Samuel wanted them to do this before he could ask the Lord to deliver them. The people of Israel quickly obeyed, and the prophet Samuel raised an altar to the Lord. From this raised altar, the Prophet Samuel cried to the Lord for the deliverance of His covenant people. God responded immediately. Suddenly, God thundered from the heavens so that He threw the Philistines into emotional and mental confusion. They were utterly discombobulated. They did not know what had hit them. Seeing a chance at victory, the children of Israel pursued them, and they fled from Israel. The Bible says the Philistines never again came into the territory of Israel all the days of Samuel. Israel also gained back the territories it had lost to the Philistines previously. So, it was a time of total restoration and victory.

VII. DAVID'S ALTAR

Then Gad [the prophet] came to David that day and said to him, "Go up, set up an altar to the Lord on the threshing floor of Araunah the Jebusite [where you saw the angel]." ¹⁹So David went up according to Gad's word, as the Lord commanded. ²⁰Araunah looked down and saw the king and his servants crossing over toward him; and he went out and bowed before the king with his face toward the ground. ²¹Araunah said, "Why has my lord the king come to his servant?" And David said, "To buy the threshing floor from you, to build an altar to the Lord, so that the plague may be held back from the people." ²²Araunah said to David, "Let my lord the king take and offer up whatever seems good to him. Look, here are oxen for the burnt offering, and threshing sledges and the yokes of the oxen for the wood. ²³All of this, O king, Araunah gives to the king." And Araunah said to the king, "May the Lord your God be favorable to you." ²⁴But the king said to Araunah, "No, but I will certainly buy it from you for a price. I will not offer burnt offerings to the Lord my God which cost me nothing." So, David purchased the threshing floor and the oxen for fifty shekels of silver. ²⁵David built an altar to the Lord there and offered burnt offerings and peace offerings. So, the Lord was moved [to compassion] by [David's] prayer for the land, and the plague was held back from Israel.

(2 Samuel 24:18-25)

One of my favorite Bible characters is the great King David. I love King David, the man after God's own heart. And yet one day, David made a colossal mistake. He chose to number the children of Israel in a census, which was against the direct commandment of the Lord given to the children of Israel by Moses, the lawgiver. David's sin aroused God's wrath to such an extent that God sent a plague among the children of Israel. Thousands died, and the death angel would have continued moving through the land had King David not listened to the Prophet Gad. The prophet told him to go and set up an altar to the Lord on the threshing floor of Araunah the Jebusite. When David arrived, Araunah, the Jebusite, was so happy to see the king that he gladly offered him the land on which he wanted to build an altar, absolutely free of charge!

However, David understood how altars work and how they are raised. He knew that he could not raise an altar to destroy a plague without paying a heavy price. The price David was going to pay for the piece of land to raise the altar was the "offering" that was needed. The Bible says, as soon as King David raised the altar and made a sacrifice unto the Lord, the plague was stopped. The land of Israel was spared from total annihilation. This passage of Scripture proves that altars are powerful platforms for destroying pandemics or plagues in a country or a generation. Christians who raise righteous altars in their homes will be protected from many diseases and pandemics that will be commonplace in the last days. It would seem to me that the name of this altar that King David raised is the "altar that ends plagues." So, it was an altar that provoked God's mercy and deliverance.

VIII. ELIJAH'S ALTAR

> At the time of the offering of the evening sacrifice, Elijah the prophet approached [the altar] and said, "O Lord, the God of Abraham, Isaac, and Israel (Jacob), let it be known today that You are God in Israel and that I am Your servant and that I have done all these things at Your word. ³⁷Answer me, O Lord, answer me, so that this people may know that You, O Lord, are God, and that You have turned their hearts back [to You]." ³⁸Then the fire of the Lord fell and consumed the burnt offering and the wood, and even the stones and the dust; it also licked up the water in the trench. ³⁹When all the people saw it, they fell face downward; and they said, "The Lord, He is God! The Lord, He is God!"
>
> (1 Kings 18:36-39)

When I traveled as a healing evangelist in South Africa, I moved around with a 1000-seat gospel tent. We saw so many miracles, signs, and wonders during those days. The Lord, in His mercy, gloriously brought many into His

Kingdom, as they gave their lives to Christ. During this time, I fell in love with the Prophet Elijah. I preached on Elijah and the prophets of Baal that sat at Jezebel's table more times than I can remember. One of my favorite messages was "The God that Answers by Fire!" This message was a direct quote of what the prophet Elijah told the children of Israel. He told them that they had to stop wavering between two opinions. He said, "If Baal was God, then follow him, but if the Lord is God, then abandon the worship of foreign deities once and for all."

He gave the people of Israel a challenge in which he said he would build an altar and place a bull on it. He was also going to allow the prophets of Jezebel to do the same. They were to call upon the name of their gods, and he was to call upon the name of the God of Israel; the God who answers by fire would be proclaimed the true and living God! The children of Israel were very excited at this proposal, and they accepted Elijah's challenge. Elijah allowed the prophets of Baal that sat at Jezebel's table to go first. After hours of pleading to Baal and cutting themselves with stones, they failed to produce supernatural fire on their evil altar. At the time of the offering of the evening sacrifice, Elijah, the prophet, approached the altar that he had raised to the God of Abraham, Isaac, and Jacob and called upon the name of the God of Israel. Shortly after his prayer, "supernatural fire" fell from heaven and consumed everything on Elijah's altar. When the children of Israel saw this, they fell on their faces and began to shout, "The Lord is God, the Lord is God!" This story proves that altars are the most powerful platforms for bringing spiritual awakening and revival to a generation. It would seem that the name of Elijah's altar is the altar of the "God who answers by fire or the altar of revival."

❧❧❧❧❧

Altars are the most powerful platforms for bringing
spiritual awakening and revival to a generation.

❧❧❧❧❧

Evil Altars

At least 39 foreign deities in the Bible are mentioned by name as the gods of the Gentile nations. Consequently, there's not enough space in this book to do an exhaustive study on all of these foreign deities. Most importantly, it is not the purpose of this writing to focus on studying foreign deities forbidden in Scripture. However, I will go through at least eight major deities and evil altars mentioned in Scripture. These foreign demonic deities very much affect us today in the 21st-century. Whereas the people of the ancient world who worshipped these deities that the Bible talks about are dead, the demonic spirits behind the worship of these idols and the erecting of evil altars never died. They just move on from one generation to the next. That is why we do well to understand this compelling subject on altars.

I.   BALAAM'S ALTAR

> *Then Balak said to Balaam, "What have you done to me? I brought you to curse my enemies, but here you have [thoroughly] blessed them instead!" [12]Balaam answered, "Must I not be obedient and careful to speak what the Lord has put in my mouth?" [13]Balak said to him, "Come with me, I implore you, to another place from where you can see them, although you will see only the nearest and not all of them; and curse them for me from there." [14]So he took Balaam to the field of Zophim to the top of [Mount] Pisgah, and built seven altars, and offered a bull and a ram on each altar.*
>
> *(Numbers 23:11-14)*

> *"For there is no enchantment or omen against Jacob, nor is there any divination against Israel. At the proper time it shall be said to Jacob And to Israel, what has God done!*
>
> *(Numbers 23:23)*

One of the most powerful witches or sorcerers mentioned in the Bible is a man named Balaam. According to the ancient book of Jasher, Baalam was a legendary worker of magic, spells, and incantations. His services in the dark arts were sought by the kings of the ancient world, from Europe to Africa. Balaam was so deep into witchcraft that his two sons Jannis and Jambres (see Exodus 7:11-22), actually challenged Moses to a duel. When Moses produced a snake supernaturally, these Chaldean sorcerers also produced their snakes. It was this same Baalam who was hired by King Balak of the Moabites to come and curse the children of Israel when they were on their way to the Promised Land. King Balak sent members of his cabinet to go and fetch this evil sorcerer so that he could conjure up curses against God's people.

However, on his way there, Balaam was intercepted by God, and an angel of God placed a divine restraining order upon him and his sorcery. The angel told Balaam that "You cannot curse what God has blessed!" So, each time Balaam tried to conjure up a curse against the children of Israel, he ended up blessing them instead! That was very frustrating for both him and King Balak, who wanted to see him conjure up a curse that could destroy the children of Israel. The altar of Balaam is the altar of sorcery, witchcraft, divination, and magic. In my meetings worldwide, especially in my crusades, I contended with the "Balaams" of this world. I saw God's power completely overpower them, and some of them even gave their lives to Christ! Glory to God! By any stretch of the imagination, the altar of witchcraft is not a righteous altar. It's an evil altar, and many have died prematurely because they were attacked by someone who stood on an altar of witchcraft. For some of you reading this book, your destiny is in a holding pattern because of a curse pronounced on your life by a witch or sorcerer! Usually, this happens because the witch or sorcerer discovered that you have something in common in your bloodline with the spirit of witchcraft.

II. JEZEBEL'S TABLE

When Ahab saw Elijah, Ahab said to him, "Are you the one who is bringing disaster on Israel?" 18Elijah said, "I have not brought disaster on Israel,

but you and your father's household have, by abandoning (rejecting) the
commandments of the Lord and by following the Baals. *¹⁹Now then, send*
word and gather to me all Israel at Mount Carmel, together with the 450
prophets of Baal and the 400 prophets of [the goddess] Asherah, who eat at
[Queen] Jezebel's table."

(1 Kings 18:17-19)

One of the most aggressive evil altars and spirits in the Bible is the table and spirit of Jezebel. We've already shown that in the Hebrew language, the words altar and table come from the same root word carrying the idea that altars are places of fellowship and food consumption. Armed with this understanding, we will not be surprised why the Apostle Paul and the apostles of Jesus admonished New Testament believers not to eat food offered to idols. That is because that's how the people of the ancient world worshipped their foreign deities at their evil altars. The 450 prophets of Baal and the 400 prophets of the goddess Asherah who ate at Jezebel's table indicate that Jezebel's table itself was an altar to the Sidonian gods she worshiped. That is why it's vital to know who is preparing your food and at what table you're fellowshipping or eating. Without a doubt, the altar of Jezebel's table was an altar of witchcraft, manipulation, and control. These were the characteristics of the infamous biblical character known as Jezebel.

III. **THE ALTAR OF BAAL**

Early the next morning when the men of the city got up, they discovered that the altar of Baal was torn down, and the Asherah which was beside it was cut down, and the second bull was offered on the altar which had been built. ²⁹So they said to one another, "Who has done this thing?" When they searched about and inquired, they were told, "Gideon the son of Joash did it." ³⁰Then the men of the city said to Joash, "Bring out your son, so that he may be executed, because he has torn down the altar of Baal and cut down the Asherah which was beside it."

(Judges 6:28-30)

According to some biblical scholars, "Baal's name" is derived from the Semitic word *ba'lu*, meaning lord. The god Baal was assumed to fulfill several significant roles by the people who worshiped him. Baal was seen as a "god of the storm, the roar of his voice in the heavens was the thunder of the sky." He was also the god who both created and granted fertility. According to folklore, Baal was the deity who was slain by enemies and thus fell into the hands of Death. It's almost a mimicking of the life of Jesus. When Baal was under the control of Death, the vegetation here on earth wilted or ceased, and procreation stopped. That is why the ancients looked to him for fertility.

He was also the god of justice, who was feared by evildoers. One might be tempted to laugh at the foolishness of the ancients, but alas, we are plagued with the same type of spiritual disease. We, too, have the propensity to bow down and worship these same worthless deities, which are nothing but demons hiding behind these idolatrous images. The worship of Baal was very common in the ancient world during the days of Jesus. According to the above passage of Scripture, Baal worship was the primary worship that caused the children of Israel to stumble and become victims of the Midianites. Thankfully, God raised Gideon and gave him the courage and grace to tear down the altar of Baal, which was in his father's house. The altar that the prophet Elijah also destroyed over the nation of Israel was Baal's.

ဏဏ~ဏ

Much of these riots (in America) are driven by
demons that are looking for expression in the souls
of men.
ဏဏ~ဏ

IV. THE ALTAR OF MOLECH (MOLOCH)

*They built the high places [for worship] of Baal in the Valley of Ben-hinnom
(son of Hinnom) to make their sons and their daughters pass through the fire
to [worship and honor] Molech—which I had not commanded them nor had
it entered My mind that they should do this repulsive thing, to cause Judah
to sin.*

(Jeremiah 32:35)

*You shall not give any of your children to offer them [by fire as a sacrifice] to
Molech [the god of the Ammonites], nor shall you profane the name of your
God [by honoring idols as gods]. I am the Lord.*

(Leviticus 18:21)

Perhaps no foreign deity and demonic entity have captured Americans' collective consciousness and that of an entire political party (the Democrats) like the altar of Molech. According to Wikipedia, Moloch (also Molech, Mollok, Milcom, or Malcam) is the biblical name of a Canaanite god associated with child sacrifice through fire or war. There is just no way to sugarcoat this; the altar of Molech is the altar driven and fueled by the sacrifice of children or the abortion of babies. As of January 10, 2020, 61 million children have been aborted in America since Roe vs. Wade went into effect.[1] Someone recently told me that this is enough blood from aborted babies to fill two football stadiums! Of those 61 million aborted babies, over 20 million are the children of Black Americans.[2] Margaret Sanger, the creator of Planned Parenthood, was a staunch believer in eugenics. According to merriamwebster.com, eugenics is defined as " the practice or advocacy of controlled selective breeding of human populations (as by sterilization) to improve the population's genetic composition. Margaret Sanger, who especially targeted the extermination of the Black race, is smiling a hellish smile from the underworld below. I will never, *ever* vote for a politician, no matter how eloquent, if they are not pro-life! Those who celebrate killing the most vulnerable among us cannot be trusted with ruling over the living. I refuse to share in the blood-guiltiness of those who promote the sacrificing of children at the altar of Molech, in the name of a "woman's right to choose!"

Sixty-one million aborted babies, by any stretch of the imagination, is a staggering number. Abortion-on-demand is the acceptable genocide of our time. Part of the curses that are swirling through America, causing much violence and blood to be spilled in her streets, is due to the senseless murder of the unborn. The Bible is very clear; this ancient god Molech was a demonic deity worshiped by child sacrifice. This is a demon that feeds on children. In America, one of the most powerful political organization and lobbying groups is Planned Parenthood. It funds most of the campaigns of Democratic politicians running for office. This satanic organization acts as a priestly agency of the altar of Molech, whether its leaders know it or not. The people who work in these clinics are nothing less than human attendants to an evil altar of death. Without a doubt, they have a lot of blood on their hands and a lot to answer for! God will hold them responsible should they die before accepting Jesus and repenting of their sins. In America, the Democratic Party is the second most important guardian and attendant to Molech's evil altar. It's so sad, and at the same time, sickening!

Before we go further, you must read this testimony of this dear sister in the Lord that was given on the Suzanne Hinn National Prayer Call on October 15, 2020.

I was a Life-long Black Democrat Until...

"Good morning, everyone. Thank you, Dr. Linda, for giving me this opportunity to share my testimony. I'll start by saying that I really didn't get why certain groups of Christians were endorsing Trump over the past few years. I was like, 'Lord, I don't get it.' I wanted Him to show me directly. So, I began to pray, and I decided to do something that I'd never done before. And that was to watch both of the political conventions. I was watching the Democratic national convention, and I believe it was on the second night. I went to bed irritated. You know it's, it's politics. And I didn't particularly care about the things that I saw and heard. And as I slept, this is where the revelation came in.

I began to physically and spiritually wrestle in my sleep. I was in and out of consciousness, just kind of, sleeping and waking up and just wrestling. In the morning, I woke up just extremely grieved as if a dark cloud was over my head. I began to pray and said to God, "What is this feeling?" And God immediately put in my spirit these words, "Don't be intoxicated." He specifically used these words, "Don't be intoxicated" by the hysteria of what's being called a historic time, with a woman of color being on the Democratic ticket. Don't be intoxicated to the point that you're distracted from what's being paraded in front of you. Look at the parade that's going by."

He went on to say, "They are using the term pro-choice; however, it's a euphemistic term. It sounds sweet and cute and all of this, but we're talking about legalized murder of the unborn. Look at how marriage is being redefined and how our children, the people's minds are being shaped to believe that this is acceptable and okay. Socialism is rearing its head and being glorified."

The Lord just went on and on how everything He calls good is being called evil, and everything that He calls evil is being called good by the Democratic Party. And He specifically spoke to my spirit at that point to say, "You cannot co-sign with this agenda." I knew that I would be directly disobeying Him if I did otherwise. I am someone who is a lifelong Democrat because I am a middle-class black woman. And I felt like that's where my vote needed to be. At that time, it still wasn't clear to me, though, to vote for Trump.

I said, "Lord, I still don't understand." Because I felt like I don't like him (Trump), I don't like his (Trump's) behavior. I began to listen to some different men of God and some different messages. One, in particular, resonated with me. This prophet of God said, "it's about the platform. It's about the agenda, and it's not about the personality." At that point, it was like an epiphany. The

Lord showed me definitively, at that point, that I'm supposed to vote for Trump, because of the platform, because of the principles that he's standing on. And then, I began to listen to the Suzanne Hinn National Prayer call, and I also came across some YouTube videos that came up in my queue of Dr. Francis Myles.

I had never heard about him previously. I started listening to messages on *issuing restraining orders and evil idols and altars*. And these messages were totally foreign to me. I had never heard these powerful concepts and the scriptural references, but they so registered with my spirit; I had just received some additional revelation at that point. I knew that I needed to take it one step further and really repent for aligning myself with evil altars by way of my vote. I began to pray, and just began to repent and confess, and denounced those wicked altars that I had previously aligned myself with and those evil agendas that I co-signed, by way of my vote.

I suddenly began to vomit. I realized at that point that there was a supernatural, demonic stronghold associated with my vote and that God had just delivered me. At that point, I said to myself, "I'll just privately go and vote, Republican. I wasn't going to say anything to anybody." But the Lord impressed me and said, "No, you can't be silent on this." So I reached out to a couple of family members and friends. This past Monday, I sent an extensive email to several family members and friends. I shared my experience because I cannot be silent on this and how critical it is for them to understand that their vote has a voice, whether they're aligned with the things of God or the things of the enemy. So, I definitely thank Dr. Myles for sharing this profound revelation knowledge, *on the Battle of Altars."* Testimony of Renissa G, **An African American Christian**

႟႟႟႟

Refuse to share in the blood-guiltiness of those who
promote the sacrificing of children at the
altar of Molech .
႟႟႟႟

V.   THE ALTAR OF ASHERAH

You shall not plant for yourself an Asherah of any kind of tree or wood beside the altar of the Lord your God, which you shall make.

(Deuteronomy 16:21)

The Asherah was a wooden symbol of a female deity that seems to have been wrongfully (and sinfully) linked with God. The people of Israel, several times over, forsook the Lord God to serve Asherah and her male demon-god counterpart, Baal. (Ashteroth is an alternative name for Asherah, Judges 2:13). Thankfully, Ashtoreth's influence over the nation of Israel was finally discredited by King Josiah. The young, zealous king "cleaned house" by destroying all the shrines erected by Solomon. It's sad that the wisest and richest man who has ever lived later turned his back on God and brought idolatry to Israel. Solomon built evil altars for all of his foreign wives.

However, King Josiah made it clear that Yahweh was the only and true God for Israel's people. Josiah killed many of the priests and priestesses of the high places, and some of them were burned on the altars they had built to these demon gods. Since the symbol of the Asherah was a pole, it is understood that this is the demonic god or goddess behind highly sensual pole dancing. The kind of pole dancing that happens in Las Vegas or in strip clubs. The goddess Asherah, or Ashteroth, was viewed by many in ancient cultures as a female counterpart to the god Baal. Consequently, she was viewed as a goddess of sex, sensuality, and fertility. There were many temple prostitutes connected to this goddess. Wherever you find people obsessed with sex or are willing to rape a woman to get sex, they are human attendants to the altar of the goddess Asherah. She was widely known for her promiscuity.

VI.   THE ALTAR OF THE GODDESS ARTEMIS (DIANA)

Now a man named Demetrius, a silversmith, who made silver shrines of [the goddess] Artemis (Diana), was bringing no small profit to the craftsmen. [25]These [craftsmen] he called together, along with the workmen of similar trades, and said, "Men, you are well aware that we make a good living from this business. ²⁶You see and hear that not only at Ephesus, but almost all over [the province of] Asia, this Paul has persuaded [people to believe his teaching] and has misled a large number of people, claiming that gods made by [human] hands are not really gods at all. ²⁷Not only is there danger that this trade of ours will be discredited, but also that the [magnificent] [g]temple of the great goddess [h]Artemis will be discredited, and that she whom all Asia and the world worship will even be dethroned and lose her glorious magnificence." ²⁸When they heard this, they were filled with rage, and they began shouting, "Great is Artemis of the Ephesians!"

(Acts 19:24-28)

Perhaps one of the most famous goddesses of the Roman Empire, or ancient Greece, was Artemis or Diana (Roman). This Greek goddess Artemis was a goddess of fertility that was worshiped in Ephesus and elsewhere during the New Testament era. A well-known statue of Artemis in Greece emphasizes her power over fertility. Paul's apostolic preaching directly challenged her worship. It precipitated a massive city-wide riot that only official representatives of the court could quell (see Acts 19:23-41. Katie and I go into more detail in our book, *Idols Riot!*)

It is interesting to note that when you look across America in 2020, there are riots in most major cities. One would think the riots are all about the issue of police brutality, but the reality is that much of these riots are driven by demons that are looking for expression in the souls of men. From this above passage of Scripture, it can be seen that the altar of the goddess Artemis or Diana is the one that is closely associated with riots! This Scripture passage would explain why college-educated people find themselves in a mob that's looting businesses and destroying property. I am convinced now, more than ever, that all riots are demonically engineered. Many of these riots are inspired by the altar of the goddess Diana (Rome) or Artemis (Greece). Thankfully, we have power and authority over these evil altars and all the idols connected to them.

VII. THE ALTAR OF DAGON

Then the Philistines took the ark of God, and they brought it from Ebenezer to [a]Ashdod. ²They took the ark of God and brought it into the house of Dagon and set it beside [the image of] Dagon [their chief idol]. ³When the people of Ashdod got up early the next day, behold, Dagon had fallen on his face on the ground before the ark of the Lord. So, they took Dagon and returned him to his place. ⁴But when they got up early the next morning, behold, Dagon had [again] fallen on his face on the ground before the ark of the Lord, and his head and both palms of his hands were [lying] cut off on the threshold; only the trunk [portion] of [the idol of] Dagon was left on him. ⁵This is the reason neither the priests of Dagon nor any who enter Dagon's house step on the threshold of Dagon in Ashdod to this day.

(1 Samuel 5:1-5)

Dagon was the highly venerated national deity of the Philistines. Each city of the Philistine pentapolis had its temple for the worship of this god. The temple statuary portraying Dagon was characterized by an upper human torso, with the lower torso of a fish. The central cultic rite in Dagon's worship was human sacrifice. When the Philistines captured the Ark of God, they took it into the temple of Dagon, their primary national deity and idol. A battle of altars immediately ensued between the two deities. The Ark of the God of Israel took the day because it was a superior altar compared to Dagon. Dagon is also known as the god of the sea and the land. That is why he was fashioned as half man and half fish. This deity is behind much of the spiritual warfare people have with water spirits or marine spirits. Marine spirits are usually the spirits that cause people (men and women) to have wet or sexual dreams.

VIII. THE ALTAR OF BEELZEBUB

Then a demon-possessed man who was blind and mute was brought to Jesus, and He healed him, so that the mute man both spoke and saw. ²³All the people wondered in amazement, and said, "Could this be the Son of David (the Messiah)?" ²⁴But the Pharisees heard it and said, "This man [a]casts out demons only by [the help of] Beelzebub (Satan) the prince of the demons." ²⁵Knowing their thoughts Jesus said to them, "Any kingdom that is divided against itself is being laid waste; and no city or house divided against itself will [continue to] stand. ²⁶If Satan casts out Satan [that is, his demons], he has become divided against himself and disunited; how then will his kingdom stand? ²⁷If I cast out the demons by [the help of] Beelzebub (Satan), by whom do your sons drive them out? For this reason, they will be your judges. ²⁸But if it is by the Spirit of God that I cast out the demons, then the Kingdom of God has come upon you [before you expected it].

(Matthew 12:22-28)

While He was on earth, Jesus was accused of operating under the power of Beelzebub, sometimes pronounced Beelzebul. Beelzebub was a Phoenician god who was worshiped at Ekron in Old Testament times (see 2 Kings 1:2-16). According to biblical scholars, the name's original meaning is unknown, but the Old Testament form, Beelzebub, means "Lord of the flies." In Jesus' day, this Phoenician god is derisively called Beelzebub, which means "lord of dung." This demonic deity is closely identified with Satan, who is the ruler of demons (see Matthew 12:24).

Jesus' enemies (the Pharisees and Sadducees) accused him of casting out demons by invoking Beelzebub (see Mark 3:22). They even accused Him of being this spirit's actual embodiment (see Matthew 10:25). Jesus rejected this foolish thinking. Instead, He pointed out that the expulsion or exorcism of demons was an announcement of Satan's defeat, heralding the arrival of God's Kingdom (see Luke 11:20-22). Jesus also told the Pharisees and the Sadducees that *"if I cast out devils by Beelzebub then what spiritual power are your children using to cast out demons?"* That pretty much shut them up. The altar of Beelzebub is closely associated with the spirit of confusion and demonic influence.

IX.   THE TOWER OF BABEL: THE ALTAR OF SELF WORSHIP

Then they said, "Come, let's build a great city for ourselves with a tower that reaches into the sky. This will make us famous and keep us from being scattered all over the world." ⁵But the Lord came down to look at the city and the tower the people were building. ⁶"Look!" he said. "The people are united, and they all speak the same language. After this, nothing they set out to do will be impossible for them! ⁷Come, let's go down and confuse the people with different languages. Then they won't be able to understand each other." ⁸In that way, the Lord scattered them all over the world, and they stopped building the city. ⁹That is why the city was called Babel, because that is where the Lord confused the people with different languages. In this way he scattered them all over the world.

(Genesis 11:4-9, NLT)

One of the most powerful evil altars to show up in Scripture was the Tower of Babel. I know many people think the Tower of Babel was simply a bunch of bored people trying to do something with their time. However, the plot behind the building of the Tower of Babel is even more sinister than that. In its very essence, the Tower of Babel was an altar to the worship of self. The entire enterprise was directed at making a name for themselves so that God did not have to scatter them across the earth to advance His Kingdom. Instead, they wanted to be together where they could make each other famous. In other words, there was nothing God-centric about the Tower of Babel. It was all about the worship of the flesh. Unfortunately, many of God's people are guilty of building the Tower of Babel, which is nothing short of the altar of self-worship. That is why people such as this can never afford to be wrong because being wrong takes self off its pedestal.

X.   CAIN'S ALTAR OF DEFIANCE

And in the course of time Cain brought to the Lord an offering of the fruit of the ground. ⁴But Abel brought [an offering of] the [finest] firstborn of his flock and the [b]fat portions. And the Lord had respect (regard) for Abel and for his offering; [5]but for Cain and his offering He had no respect. So Cain became extremely angry (indignant), and [c]he looked annoyed and hostile. [6]And the Lord said to Cain, "Why are you so angry? And why do you look annoyed? [7]If you do well [believing Me and doing what is acceptable and pleasing to Me], will you not be accepted? And if you do not do well [but ignore My instruction], sin crouches at your door; its desire is for you [to overpower you], but you must master it." [8]Cain talked with Abel his brother [about what God had said]. And when they were [alone, working] in the field, Cain [d]attacked Abel his brother and killed him.

(Genesis 4:3-8)

Among the evil altars that we have studied, there is none that I find more unbelievable than Cain's altar of defiance. What is of note is that the two sons of Adam and Eve had most certainly been told about the technology of altars by their father, Adam. They both knew what it would take to engage with God. I'm almost certain Adam told his sons what the Lord God required: blood for the atonement of sin. Instead, in utter defiance, Cain brought an offering of the fruit of the ground even though God himself had already cursed the ground in Genesis Chapter 3. Why would he offer God an offering on his altar from produce coming from the ground that was already under a curse? Inevitably God did not respond favorably to Cain's offering; however, God did look favorably on Abel's offering. Abel gave God exactly what He asked for to affect the atonement of the soul - a sacrifice of blood!

PRAYER OF ACTIVATION!

"Heavenly Father, I ask for the Court of Heaven to be seated and for the books of my destiny to be opened as I come before the Judge of all the earth to plead my case against any evil altar in my life or bloodline that is speaking against me. I decree and declare that the Holy Spirit is my official guide and counselor in this courtroom. Heavenly Father, I surrender all rights to self-representation; instead, I ask my defense attorney and mediator of the new covenant, the Lord Jesus Christ, to represent me in your Royal Courtroom against all idols and evil altars that are controlling my life and bloodline, in any way. I also ask the Lord Jesus to heal me by His blood from all soul wounds caused by idols and evil altars in my bloodline. I am seeking a verdict of release from the power of these evil altars in Jesus' Name.

I now enter a plea of 'guilty' into the court's records concerning any legitimate accusations that Satan has filed in Court against me or my bloodline. For Jesus said, in Matthew 5:25, *"Come to terms quickly [at the earliest opportunity] with your opponent at law while you are with him on the way [to court], so that your opponent does not hand you over to the judge, and the judge to the guard, and you are thrown into prison."* Lord, since I am under oath, I cannot lie about my sinful activities and the iniquities of my bloodline that are connected to idolatry and the erecting evil altars. I repent for all sins and transgressions that I and my ancestors ever committed against you and the laws of nature. Cleanse me from all sin by the blood of Jesus, according to 1 John 1:9. I now formally submit my guilty plea and repentance to the court, in Jesus' Name."

Heavenly Father,

- I decree and declare that the Spirit of God is establishing godly altars in my life while destroying every evil altar, which is calling my name, in Jesus' Name!
- I decree and declare that I loose the power of Noah's altar in my life, which caused God to reverse a curse in Jesus' Name!
- I decree and declare that I loose the power of Abraham's altar in my life, which caused him to possess the land the Lord had promised him, in Jesus' Name!
- I decree and declare that I loose the power of the altar of Mount Moriah, which caused Abraham to sacrifice Isaac in total obedience to God, in Jesus' Name!
- I decree and declare that I loose the power of David's altar in my life, which caused God to stop a nationwide pandemic, in Jesus' Name!
- I decree and declare that I loose God's supernatural fire against the evil altars of Baal, Molech, and Jezebel, in Jesus' Name!
- I decree and declare that the altar of self-worship in my life and bloodline is completely destroyed, in Jesus' Name!

LIFE APPLICATION

SECTION

Memory Verse

They built the high places [for worship] of Baal in the Valley of Ben-hinnom (son of Hinnom) to make their sons and their daughters pass through the fire to [worship and honor] Molech—which I had not commanded them nor had it entered My mind that they should do this repulsive thing, to cause Judah to sin.

(Jeremiah 32:35)

Reflections

1. What was wrong with the altar Cain built for the Lord?

2. What happened on the altar Abraham built to the Lord on Mount Moriah?

5

The 12 Laws of an Altar

The law of the Lord is perfect (flawless), restoring and refreshing the soul;
The statutes of the Lord are reliable and trustworthy, making wise the simple.

(Psalms 19:7)

God designed creation to revolve around a set of fixed laws. By definition, "laws" are principles, protocols, and regulations designed to govern society's proper functioning, systems, and disciplines. For example, whenever you buy an appliance from any manufacturer, it comes with a user's manual. This user's manual is also known as the manufacturer's protocols (laws) that govern the product, regulate its proper use, and stipulate actions that would abuse its normal usage and endanger the end-user. Unfortunately, very few end-users take the time to read the manufacturer's manual. Nevertheless, to get the most out of any product, we must obey the manufacturer's laws governing the product. This chapter will introduce you to laws introduced by the manufacturer (God) that govern all altars, whether godly or evil!

> **Every altar requires a human attendant, all altars are places of covenant, and every altar is fueled or powered by the sacrifice or offering of its human attendant.**

1. **ALL ALTARS HAVE A DEDICATED HUMAN ATTENDANT.**

And behold, there came a man of God out of Judah by the word of the Lord to Bethel. Jeroboam stood by the altar to burn incense. ²The man cried against the altar by the word of the Lord, O altar, altar, thus says the Lord: Behold, a son shall be born to the house of David, Josiah by name; and on you shall he offer the priests of the high places who burn incense on you, and men's bones shall be burned on you.

(1 Kings 13:1-2)

As a consequence of the Law of Dominion/Territory, all altars, without exception, require a human attendant. By definition, a human is a spirit being housed in a physical body of dirt. That is why when people die, they essentially lose their humanity (physicalness) and become spirit-beings just like angels and demons. When this happens, these "former humans" suddenly become illegal on earth. They graduate to their heavenly home if they accepted Messiah-Jesus as their Lord and Savior. If they rejected Messiah-Jesus, they are dragged to hell by the idols (demon-gods) they worshipped while they were on earth.

That explains why God strictly forbade the children of Israel to fraternize with necromancers. Necromancers are spiritual mediums that specialize in the demonic art of talking to the dead. In Isaiah 8:19, the prophet declares, *"When the people [instead of trusting God] say to you, "Consult the mediums [who try to talk to the dead] and the soothsayers who chirp and whisper and mutter," should not a people consult their God? Should they consult the dead-on behalf of the living?"* That also explains why "idols (demons) riot" when they lose control of a human being. You will never again see the great Billy Graham, Ravi Zacharias, or Reinhard Bonke preach to a stadium full of humans because they lost their humanness when they died and lost their physical bodies of dirt. That is why mankind's final redemptive gift from God is the "redemption of the body!"

2. ALL ALTARS HAVE A GUIDING OR SUPERVISING SPIRIT.

> *That night the Lord said to Gideon, Take your father's bull, the second bull seven years old, and pull down the altar of Baal that your father has and cut down the Asherah [symbol of the goddess Asherah] that is beside it;*
>
> *(Judges 6:25)*

There is no altar without a guiding or supervising spirit that oversees the altar. That is another reason why God forbids His people from having idols in their lives. When we allow idols, which are essentially demons, to build altars in our souls, these demon-gods become the guiding spirits in our lives. The influence of these idols is why there are times when Christians struggle with sinful passions that have nothing to do with the character of Christ. Suddenly, you want to smoke a cigarette; you want to get drunk; for some, the desire to sleep with a person who is not their spouse suddenly becomes almost overbearing. Who is guiding the soul into wanting things? It is the idols and the evil altars we have built for them in our souls. My friend Katie Souza calls these illicit desires and impulses "idols rioting!" If you have not read our book *Idols Riot*, I encourage you to take a moment right now and buy this book on Amazon or iBooks. It is a companion book to the one you're reading now. It will give you a full scope on how to prosecute idols and the evil altars in the Courts of Heaven.

3. ALL ALTARS ARE POWERED BY THE SACRIFICE (S) OF THE HUMAN ATTENDANT (S) WHO SERVICES THE ALTAR.

> *But King David said to Araunah, No, but I will buy it of you for a price. I will not offer burnt offerings to the Lord my God of that which costs me nothing. So David bought the threshing floor and the oxen for fifty shekels*

of silver. ²⁵David built there an altar to the Lord and offered burnt offerings and peace offerings. So the Lord heeded the prayers for the land, and Israel's plague was stayed.

(2 Samuel 24:24-25)

Without fail, all altars are places of sacrifice. God, or the demonic gods behind the altar, demands that the human attendants demonstrate their commitment and loyalty to the deity behind the altar. That is why all biblical godly altars were covered with the blood of animals slaughtered in sacrifice to the God of Israel. The altar of the Lord also demanded other types of offerings, such as peace offerings, first-fruits, tithes, alms, and so forth. Since the devil is a master copycat, his evil altars also demand sacrifice from the human attendants who have allowed these demon-gods to build altars in their soul or bloodline.

4. **ALL ATTENDANTS TO AN ALTAR ARE FED BY OR PROVIDED FOR BY THE ALTAR THEY SERVE.**

Do you not know that those men who are employed in the services of the temple get their food from the temple? And that those who tend the altar share with the altar [in the offerings brought]?

(1 Corinthians 9:13)

There is another important aspect that governs all altars. All attendants to an altar receive their food or provision from God or the demon-god over the altar they serve. In the sixth chapter of Matthew's gospel, Jesus admonished his disciples not to worry about what they are going to eat or what they will wear. Why? Jesus knew this principle of altars. Most importantly, the menu at any altar is determined by God or the idol (demon-god) behind the altar.

That is why an attendant to the altar of the LORD feeds on righteousness, peace, joy, love, godly prosperity, long-suffering, and so forth. However, any attendant to the altar of an idol also eats what the demon-god eats. Consequently, if the idol is a demon of sexual perversion, the attendant will feast on pornography, fornication, adultery, masturbation, even pedophilia in certain instances. Why? Because according to the law of altars, God, or the idol behind the altar, determines the menu. One of the quickest ways to determine whether a person is serving God or an idol is to note what they are addicted to. An addict is simply a human attendant to an altar of addiction in their soul, so when the idol behind the altar is hungry, these people will start looking for the food (drugs, alcohol, heroin or gambling, etc.) the idol eats. The idol will riot to such an extent that these people will not rest until the idol is fed!

5. **ALL ALTARS ARE PLACES OF RITUAL (PERPETUAL OR REPETITIVE ACTIVITY).**

> *Do not be carried about by different and varied and alien teachings; for it is good for the heart to be established and ennobled and strengthened by means of grace (God's favor and spiritual blessing) and not [to be devoted to] foods [rules of diet and ritualistic meals], which bring no [spiritual] benefit or profit to those who observe them.* [10] *We have an altar from which those who serve and worship in the tabernacle have no right to eat.*
>
> (Hebrews 13:9-10)

We serve a God who is a genius at setting the correct background for the revelation He wants you to master. I was born in Africa, where we were confronted with altars long before we came to Christ. I do not have some of the theological hang-ups some Christians in the West seem to have when it comes to the subject of altars. I know that the subject of altars cannot be relegated to the Old Testament and thrown into the dust bins of history. Altars are critical components for connecting the earth to the deity you serve. One of the things I noticed growing up in Africa is that all altars are places of ritual. According to dictionary.com, the word ritual is defined as "an established or prescribed procedure for a religious or other rite." The ritual behind any altar can be quickly discerned by examining the repetitive cycles in people's lives. For instance, King David was an avid worshipper of God, so what was the repetitive ritual in his life? Let's him tell it in Psalms 34:1, *"Lord! I'm bursting with joy over what you've done for me! My lips are full of perpetual praise."*

So how can you use this aspect of altars to discern the number of idols operating in your soul or bloodline? Take inventory of repetitive cycles of behavior or happenings in your life that violate or compete with Messiah-Jesus. For instance, do you find that for one reason or the other, you blow up in anger, repent in the aftermath, only to do it again and again and again? Do you know what you are? You are an attendant to an idol and altar of anger or rage. That is why you can't control yourself until you allow the Holy Spirit to divorce you from the idol and destroy its altar in your soul. The Body of Christ is full of born-again Christians who love Messiah-Jesus but struggle with so many idols in their soul or bloodline. Just look at the rituals (repetitive behaviors) in their lives that they clearly have no control over.

6.   **All altars speak (whether they are stationary or mobile.)**

> *A devout man who venerated God and treated Him with reverential obedience, as did all his household; and he gave much alms to the people and prayed continually to God. ³About the ninth hour (about 3:00 p.m.) of the day he saw clearly in a vision an angel of God entering and saying to him, Cornelius! ⁴And he, gazing intently at him, became frightened and said, what is it, Lord? And the angel said to him, your prayers and your [generous] gifts to the poor have come up [as a sacrifice] to God and have been remembered by Him.*
>
> *(Acts 10:2-4)*

All altars speak, whether they are stationary or mobile. What do I mean by this? Since all altars are power stations, places of exchange, and landing strips for God, holy angels, or demonic-gods, altars can speak on behalf of the human attendant. In the case of Cornelius, the Roman centurion who built an altar of devotion to God by continually giving alms to the poor and praying daily, the altar began to speak in his favor in the Courts of Heaven. Suddenly an angel from God showed up in his house. The angel told him that his alms and praying had come before God as a memorial. The angel proceeded to tell him to go and get Peter, who was in Joppa, a neighboring town. When the Apostle Peter arrived, the Holy Ghost fell upon Cornelius and his entire family. They were gloriously saved and filled with the Holy Ghost. The altar of the Lord in his life had spoken for him and brought him and his family into the Kingdom.

However, the voice of the altars of demons (idols) has a malicious agenda that lines up with Satan's character to kill, steal, and destroy (John 10:10). So how do you recognize the voice of the idol or evil altar in your soul? Get into a quiet place and try to spend intimate time with the Lord. It won't be long before you begin to hear voices in your heart and mind reminding or telling you about things you need to do or should be doing. All of a sudden, these thoughts appear in your mind: "I wonder if there are any notifications or messages for me on Facebook? Do we have tomatoes or onions in the fridge? I wonder if the new Avengers movie is out? Why am I having such strong sexual thoughts or desires for this person when I'm trying to spend time with the Lord? I need to go to Ross or Dillard's and do some shopping before the 50-percent off sale ends."

Have you ever asked yourself why it is so difficult for you to concentrate on the Lord during your quiet time with Him? Most importantly, what is the source of all of these questions? They are the voices of the idols and evil altars in your soul or bloodline projected onto the screen of your mind. The altars are speaking by the idols in your soul or bloodline. Essentially the idols in your soul or bloodline go on a violent riot every time you choose to spend intimate time with the Lord in prayer. They know this is a dangerous time for them because you might just recognize them and cry to the Lord to deliver you!

⋙⋙⋙

The voice of the altars of demons (idols) has a malicious agenda that lines up with the character of Satan to kill, steal and destroy

⋙⋙⋙

7.   ALL ALTARS ARE PLACES OF EXCHANGE.

And Noah built an altar to the Lord and took of every clean [four-footed] animal and of every clean fowl or bird and offered burnt offerings on the altar. [21]When the Lord smelled the pleasing odor [a scent of satisfaction to His heart], the Lord said to Himself, I will never again curse the ground because of man, for the imagination (the strong desire) of man's heart is evil and wicked from his youth; neither will I ever again smite and destroy every living thing, as I have done.

(Genesis 8:20-21)

All altars are places of exchange. Growing up in Africa, I noticed that each time our parents or grandparents took us to a witch doctor to inquire from the gods, these witch doctors would demand an exchange on behalf of the idol. In one case, we were required to bring two chickens to the witch doctor before he could speak to us. After the exchange, the witch doctor would inquire from the idol and tell us what we needed to do to get healed, prosper, get married, have children, or destroy one of our enemies. Imagine my pleasant surprise when I discovered that what African witch doctors were doing was actually based upon an ancient biblical pattern, except for the fact that as messengers of Satan, they twisted the purpose of altars to serve the agenda of demons. I discovered that in the Bible, God made it very clear to the children of Israel that altars are places of exchange. In the above passage of Scripture, Noah built an altar to the LORD, and he gave God an offering of every clean [four-footed] animal and of every clean fowl or bird. In exchange, God made a vow never again to curse the ground because of man, nor destroy the earth with a flood.

True to form, the devil is a master copycat. He also demands an exchange from human attendants who have idols and evil altars in their souls or bloodlines. As a result, many end-up exchanging their soul's eternal security for power, fame, and money in this life. Listen to what Satan told Jesus during His wilderness experience, according to Matthew 4:8-9., *"And the third time the accuser lifted Jesus up into a very high mountain range and showed him all the kingdoms of the world and all the splendor that goes with it. "All of these kingdoms I will give to you," the accuser said, "if only you will kneel down before me and worship me."* We must get rid of the idols in our soul or bloodline. Until we do, they will demand an exchange from us. Pastors, politicians, and businessmen have lost their influence and position because the "idol of sexual perversion" in their lives demanded an exchange – such as sex with young boys instead of sex with their wives. The idol then exposed them to public shame and took everything they had. Checkmate! That was a pricey exchange! As you read this book, ask yourself this question: What exchanges do you keep having in your life?

8. **ALL ALTARS ARE PLACES OF COVENANT.**

> *When they came to the place of which God had told him, Abraham built an altar there; then he laid the wood in order and bound Isaac his son and laid him on the altar on the wood. [15]The Angel of the Lord called to Abraham from heaven a second time [16]And said, I have sworn by Myself, says the Lord, that since you have done this and have not withheld [from Me] or begrudged [giving Me] your son, your only son, [17]In blessing I will bless you and in multiplying I will multiply your descendants like the stars of the heavens and like the sand on the seashore. And your Seed (Heir) will possess the gate of His enemies, [18]And in your Seed [Christ] shall all the nations of the earth be blessed and [by Him] bless themselves, because you have heard and obeyed My voice.*
>
> *(Genesis 22:9, 15-18)*

All altars are places of agreement or covenant. They are places of meeting where humanity meets with divinity to enter into legal and covenantal agreements that are, in most cases, multi-generational. When Abraham demonstrated his total obedience and loyalty to God at an altar by his willingness to sacrifice his son, Isaac, God entered into a living covenant with him. So, we can safely say that all covenants, whether they are righteous or evil, are sustained on and by altars. Covenants are impossible to sustain without altars, so, before you can break a demonic covenant over a person's life, it behooves you to understand the altar that the covenant stands on.

9. **ALL ALTARS CAN HEAR.**

> *The man cried against the altar by the word of the Lord, O altar, altar, thus*
> *says the Lord: Behold, a son shall be born to the house of David, Josiah by*
> *name; and on you shall he offer the priests of the high places who burn incense*
> *on you, and men's bones shall be burned on you.*
>
> (1 Kings 13:2)

If I have learned anything from God, it is that there are no meaningless details in Scripture. In the above passage, a nameless prophet of God is sent to Bethel to prophesy against the altar in Bethel. In the prophecy, the prophet of God addresses the evil altar directly and says, *"O altar, altar, thus says the Lord: Behold, a son shall be born to the house of David, Josiah by name; and on you shall he offer the priests of the high places who burn incense on you, and men's bones shall be burned on you."* The million-dollar question is, "Why is he talking to an altar if the altar cannot hear his voice." The answer is simple; all altars can hear because all altars are alive.

All altars alive either through God or through the idol (demon-god) that powers the altar. So, when you speak to an altar, you are actually addressing God or the idol that the altar belongs to. That is what God was doing through the nameless prophet. The Lord spoke to me and said, "Francis, the evidence of hearing is an accurate response. If something has heard you then, it must do exactly what is asked." What happened to the altar at Bethel that the prophet spoke to? It broke apart, and its ashes were poured out according to the word of the prophet. In other words, both the idol (the demon-god) and the altar heard the word of the Lord at the same time.

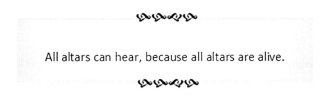

All altars can hear, because all altars are alive.

10. **ALL ALTARS EITHER HAVE GOD OR AN IDOL (DEMON-GOD) THAT IS WORSHIPPED ON THE ALTAR.**

Then the Lord appeared to Abram and said, I will give this land to your posterity. So, Abram built an altar there to the Lord, who had appeared to him.

(Genesis 12:7)

Then Solomon built a high place for Chemosh the abominable idol of Moab, on the hill opposite Jerusalem, and for Molech the abominable idol of the Ammonites. 8 And he did so for all of his foreign wives, who burned incense and sacrificed to their gods.

(1 Kings 11:7)

One of the things you must never forget is that ultimately altars are places of worship. Worship is the number one activity of altars. Why? Because we were created for God's pleasure. Worship is how we celebrate God and demonstrate our allegiance and devotion to Him. Since the devil has always wanted to be like God, he also ruthlessly demands worship from his followers. Because altars are places of worship, God declares emphatically, *"Thou shall have no other gods before me!"* Coincidentally, this is the first commandment. So, when we have idols and the evil altars dedicated to them in our soul or bloodline, we will find ourselves in those compromised areas of our lives, worshiping demons instead of the living God. The Body of Christ must understand this message on altars.

11. **SPIRITUAL WARFARE IS THE RESULT OF TWO OPPOSING ALTARS STANDING SIDE BY SIDE.**

The Philistines brought the ark of God from Ebenezer to Ashdod. ²They took the ark of God into the house of Dagon and set it beside Dagon [their idol]. ³When they of Ashdod arose early on the morrow, behold, Dagon had fallen

upon his face on the ground before the ark of the Lord. So, they took Dagon
and set him in his place again.

1 Samuel 5:1-2)

I am sure every follower of Messiah-Jesus knows that the Bible says we are involved in high-stakes spiritual warfare between the Kingdom of Light and the forces of darkness. The Lord recently showed me that what we call spiritual warfare is nothing short of the battle that ensues when an altar from God's Kingdom of Light is placed next to an altar from the kingdom of darkness. The close proximity and the fact that no two altars can occupy the same space result in spiritual warfare. In the above passage of Scripture, the Philistines brought the Ark of God from Ebenezer to Ashdod. Upon their arrival, they took the Ark of God into the house of Dagon, and they set the Ark of God next to this idol.

When they woke up the following morning, Dagon was lying on the floor with his face looking at the ground. The Ark of God, which was the altar of the Lord in Israel, was pronouncing its supremacy over the idol of the Philistines. Have you ever wondered why some people on your new job disliked you on your first day of employment even though you had never interacted with them before? It's not personal; it's simply the inevitable battle of altars. The idols and evil altars in their soul fight against the altar of the Lord in your soul. Unfortunately, this same phenomenon takes place within the souls of believers who love the Lord Jesus but have idols in their souls. They have yet to surrender to the LORD. They find themselves in constant spiritual turmoil in their will, mind, and emotions, as they struggle between the righteous demands of the altar of the Lord and the evil desires of the idols and evil altars in their soul or bloodline. This book is a divine prescription for deliverance.

12. WHOEVER CARRIES THE SUPERIOR ALTAR TAKES THE DAY!

But when they arose early the next morning, behold, Dagon had again fallen
on his face on the ground before the ark of the Lord, and [his] head and both
the palms of his hands were lying cut off on the threshold; only the trunk of
Dagon was left him. ⁵This is the reason neither the priests of Dagon nor any

who come into Dagon's house tread on the threshold of Dagon in Ashdod to this day. [6]But the hand of the Lord was heavy upon the people of Ashdod, and He caused [mice to spring up and there was] very deadly destruction and He smote the people with [very painful] tumors or boils, both Ashdod and its territory. [7]When the men of Ashdod saw that it was so, they said, the ark of the God of Israel must not remain with us, for His hand is heavy on us and on Dagon our god.

(1 Samuel 5:4-7)

According to the 12th law, whoever carries the superior altar takes the day! What does this statement mean? It means that to be delivered from the power of an evil altar, we must strengthen the altar of the Lord in our lives. The altar of the Lord in our own lives must become stronger than the idol and evil altar we are trying to destroy. In the above passage of Scripture, when the Philistines brought the Ark of God into the house of Dagon, they did not understand this 12th Law of Altars. But God did! So, He wasted no time demonstrating that the altar of the Ark of God was more superior to the altar of the idol, Dagon. When the Philistines found Dagon lying on the ground, they did not get the message. So, they propped up the idol and set it once again next to the Ark of God.

When they returned the second day, Dagon was lying on the floor with its head and the palms of its hands broken! This time they got the message, and it terrified them. The moral of the story is clear. Whoever carries the superior altar takes the day! If you want the Lord to deliver you from the power of the idols and evil altars in your bloodline, you must practice spiritual disciplines like praying and fasting. Prayer and fasting will starve the idols in your soul while strengthening your spirit man to be more connected to the Lord.

Whoever has the superior altar rules the day!

PRAYER OF ACTIVATION!

"Heavenly Father, I ask for the Court of Heaven to be seated and for the books of my destiny to be opened as I come before the Judge of all the earth to plead my case against any evil altar in my life or bloodline that is speaking against me. I decree and declare that the Holy Spirit is my official guide and counselor in this courtroom. Heavenly Father, I surrender all rights to self-representation; instead, I ask my defense attorney and mediator of the new covenant, the Lord Jesus Christ, to represent me in your Royal Courtroom against all idols and evil altars that are controlling my life and bloodline, in any way. I also ask the Lord Jesus to heal me by His blood from all soul wounds caused by idols and evil altars in my bloodline. I am seeking a verdict of release from the power of these evil altars, in Jesus' name.

I now enter a plea of 'guilty' into the court's records concerning any legitimate accusations that Satan has filed in Court against me or my bloodline. For Jesus said, in Matthew 5:25, *"Come to terms quickly [at the earliest opportunity] with your opponent at law while you are with him on the way [to court], so that your opponent does not hand you over to the judge, and the judge to the guard, and you are thrown into prison."* Lord, since I am under oath, I cannot lie about my sinful activities and the iniquities of my bloodline that are connected to idolatry and the erecting evil altars. I repent for all sins and transgressions that I and my ancestors ever committed against you and the laws of nature. Cleanse me from all sin by the blood of Jesus, according to 1 John 1:9. I now formally submit my guilty plea and repentance to the court, in Jesus' Name."

Heavenly Father

- I decree and declare that every human attendant to evil altars that are speaking against me are completely bound, in Jesus' Name!
- I decree and declare that every supervising spirit to an evil altar that is speaking against me is completely bound, in Jesus' Name!
- I decree and declare that every evil sacrifice on altars that are working against me is destroyed in Jesus' Name!
- I decree and declare that everything that I have been fed in my dreams from evil altars will have no adverse effect on me, in Jesus' Name!
- I decree and declare that God is setting me free from every addictive or controlling evil ritual in my life in Jesus' Name!
- I decree and declare that I am completely healed from all soul wounds, which have connected me to evil altars, in Jesus' Name!
- I decree and declare that the Holy Spirit is arresting every stationary or mobile evil altar, which is working against me, in Jesus' Name!

LIFE APPLICATION
SECTION

Memory Verse

And behold, there came a man of God out of Judah by the word of the Lord to Bethel. Jeroboam stood by the altar to burn incense. 2 The man cried against the altar by the word of the Lord, O altar, altar, thus says the Lord: Behold, a son shall be born to the house of David, Josiah by name; and on you shall he offer the priests of the high places who burn incense on you, and men's bones shall be burned on you.

(1 Kings 13:1-2)

Reflections

1. Why do altars require a dedicated human attendant?

   _____

   _____

   _____

   _____

2. What is the connection between the human attendant and supervising spirit over the altar?

   _____

   _____

   _____

   _____

All altars are places of exchange!

6

Overthrowing the Altar of Your Father's House

That night the Lord said to Gideon, Take your father's bull, the second bull seven years old, and pull down the altar of Baal that your father has and cut down the Asherah [symbol of the goddess Asherah] that is beside it; 26 And build an altar to the Lord your God on top of this stronghold with stones laid in proper order. Then take the second bull and offer a burnt sacrifice with the wood of the Asherah which you shall cut down.

(Judges 6:25-26)

Without a shadow of a doubt, the most difficult fight you will ever face in your life with idols and evil altars in your bloodline is when the LORD sends you to tear down the evil altars of your father's house, to dethrone the idol (demon-god) that sits on it! Be warned! Why? Because your forefathers (those in authority) built the altars for the idols (familiar spirits), permitting them to reside in your bloodline. The decisions they made over the family became legally binding in the spirit realm and are therefore recognized in the Courts of Heaven. Deceived by the devil, many of our forefathers willingly opened the door of the family lineage to the idols (familiar spirits) and evil altars that are now firmly planted in your generational ancestry.

In his analysis of Gideon's story in Judges 6, Lance Walnau tells us, "his nation and family suffered severely for seven years because of idolatry toward Baal. He tore down a family Baal altar (his father's altar) and built-in its place an altar to the Lord and sacrificed a bull on it. This started a cycle of deliverance in others. The men of the city were livid when they saw the altar turned down. But that anger wasn't of them; it was the dispossessed Baal spirit working through them. The devil will attack you through people when he is under attack through your obedience to God."[1] (Excerpt from "Alter the Altar and Break the Curse Article" by Lance Walnau[1])

Every Family Needs a Deliverer!

There seems to be a redemptive thread that runs throughout the Scriptures, and it is this: God always raises a deliverer in families. I believe many of you reading this book are doing so because you carry the anointing to completely deliver your family from the familiar spirits and the evil altars from which they operate in your bloodline.

In Semitic tradition, God did not usually make a covenant with the sons while their fathers were alive. So, why did God go to Gideon to destroy Baal's evil altar in his father's house? The answer lies in understanding who Gideon's father was. Gideon's father was, in fact, the high priest to the altar of Baal. He, among many others, was responsible for corrupting the nation of Israel with the idolatrous worship of this Canaanite deity. Gideon's father had a lot in common with the evil altar from which this demon functioned since he's the one who serviced the altar every day. Do you remember in John's gospel when Jesus said, *"The prince of this world cometh but he has nothing in me?"* Jesus was teaching as a very powerful warfare principle for taking back territory from the enemy's hands. *I will not speak with you much longer, for the ruler of the world (Satan) is coming. And he has no claim on Me [no power over Me nor anything that he can use against Me]. (John 14:30)*

It's quite difficult, if not altogether impossible, to overthrow a demon or an evil altar with which you have much in common. It's difficult to deliver anyone from a demon they love. Knowing this, the Lord bypassed Gideon's father and went straight to his son to make him the family deliverer. Even though Gideon was the son of the high priest to Baal, it would seem that he was a very reluctant follower at best. When the Angel of God touched Gideon's life, Gideon began to talk to the angel about all the stories of God delivering the nation of Israel from Egypt and about the miracles He had performed for His people, Israel. Most likely, in his private time, Gideon spent a lot of time wishing he knew the God of his forefathers, Abraham, Isaac, and Jacob, more intimately. No wonder God chose him as a candidate to destroy the evil altars of his father's house. Many of you that are reading this book can testify that you have always been the black sheep of the family or the "odd-one-out," looking for God while the rest of your family was busy chasing the world! Is it any wonder that God has chosen you to be the "Moses or Gideon" of your family? God is going to use you to tear down and uproot demonic altars that have been in your bloodline for generations.

❧❧❧❧❧

Deceived by the devil, many of our forefathers
willingly opened the door to the family bloodline to
the idols
❧❧❧❧❧

Obeying Scared!

Then Gideon took ten men of his servants and did as the Lord had told him, but because he was too afraid of his father's household and the men of the city to do it by day, he did it by night. [28] And when the men of the city arose early in the morning, behold, the altar of Baal was cast down, and the Asherah was cut down that was beside it, and the second bull was offered on the altar which had been built.

(Judges 6:27-28)

We have to get this idea out of our minds that obeying God is always fun and easy. It's my experience that obeying God is the right thing to do, always, but boy, it is never easy! So, many times in my life, I've had to obey God scared! It's my prayer that you will quickly learn the art of obeying God scared. Many of the heroes of the faith that we look up to really had to obey God scared. I don't think for one second; it was easy for the prophet Elijah to go and confront Jezebel and her 450 prophets of Baal in their territory. But he did it anyway! The result was a sweeping nationwide revival after he slaughtered all the 450 prophets of Baal, who ate at Jezebel's table.

When the Lord told Gideon to tear down the altar of his father's house, he was terrified! The reason he was terrified was obvious. God was asking him to literally dismantle his father's business, for attending to Baal was his father's business. Most important, the idol Baal and its evil altar was a familiar spirit, which was very acquainted with him. It knew Gideon's fears, weaknesses, and soulish propensities. Gideon was probably born under the influence of this spirit because his father was Baal's high priest in the land. On top of this, Gideon respected his father and wanted to do his best to be a good son. He wanted to honor his father and not bring him shame. But deep down in his heart, he knew that if he did not obey God, his destiny would be stalled, and the spirit of Baal and its evil altar would continue to control his entire bloodline. So, he chose to obey God, scared!

Get Ready for a Push-Back!

And they said to one another, Who has done this thing? And when they searched and asked, they were told, Gideon son of Joash has done this thing. [30]Then the men of the city commanded Joash, Bring out your son, that he may die, for he has pulled down the altar of Baal and cut down the Asherah beside it. [31]But Joash said to all who stood against him, Will you contend for Baal? Or will you save him? He who will contend for Baal, let him be put to death while it is still morning. If Baal is a god, let him contend for himself because one has pulled down his altar. ³²Therefore on that day he called Gideon Jerubbaal, meaning, Let Baal contend against him, because he had pulled down his altar.

(Judges 6:27-32)

The idol and evil altar of your father's house is so firmly rooted in your ancestral bloodline that some members of your family even behave like the idol. The idol in this scenario is the familiar spirit assigned to your bloodline. So, when God sends you to bring down the idol and evil altar of your father's house, get ready for a severe push-back! Get ready for some family members to rise like remote-controlled zombies to attack you for no apparent reason. Don't take this personally, and don't get your feelings hurt. They are just animating the anger and fear of the idol and evil altar of your father's house that knows that God has anointed you to dethrone it!

Gideon had no struggle building a personal altar of consecration to the Lord. However, as soon as God told him to tear down the evil altar of his father's house, a spirit of fear and intimidation came upon him. God told him to tear down the evil altar of his father's house in broad daylight, but as we have already noted, he was terrified. Instead, he went at night and took ten of his father's servants with him so they could help him get the job done. The moral of this story is that God doesn't care if you tear down the evil altar of your father's house in broad daylight or at night with a bunch of like-minded intercessors helping you. Just do it! Getting it done is all that matters!

The Prophetic Dream that Changed My Family!

[One may hear God's voice] in a dream, in a vision of the night, when deep sleep falls on men while slumbering upon the bed, ¹⁶Then He opens the ears of men and seals their instruction [terrifying them with warnings], ¹⁷That He may withdraw man from his purpose and cut off pride from him [disgusting him with his own disappointing self-sufficiency]. ¹⁸He holds him back from

the pit [of destruction], and his life from perishing by the sword [of God's destructive judgments].

(Job 33:15-18)

Something supernatural and life-changing happened to me and my entire family. It fits perfectly in this chapter, so I will tell you about it! My dear mother, Ester, died and went to be with Jesus in May of 2015. My father, Daniel, followed her to heaven a year later. She was my best friend, and I mourned her deeply. I mention her heavenly transition only to give you context concerning the prophetic dream God gave my sister Judith in 2018, which shifted everything in our family, including the projection of my ministry! I will let my sister Judy tell it in her own words.

"I greet you all in Jesus' name. My beloved ones, this is a dream I had after reading the book, *Issuing Divine Restraining Orders from the Courts of Heaven* by Dr. Francis Myles.

In my dream, I found myself in Ndola, standing near our family house. I was wondering what I was doing there. Suddenly I saw a woman running towards me. She was telling me something I couldn't understand. As I was trying to catch what she was saying, I heard a voice behind me. It was Mum's voice. She told me not to listen to the other woman. Mum then gave me an old, thick book that had old, dirty pages. She told me to burn the book. "This is the book that contains all the bad things that were spoken over our family." Mum declared. She then told me to extend my right hand, which I did. She handed me a new green book. It looked like a diary. She said to me, "This book is where all the good things God intended for our family are written."

When I lifted my face, I found myself inside our Ndola family house inside the girls' bedroom. I heard a knock on the window. When I opened it, Emmanuel (my brother) was telling me to open the door for him. I went out of the bedroom to the sitting room where I found a lot of Dad's relatives sleeping. I was very upset, and I said to myself, "Why don't you leave us alone? Even when Dad has died, you are still following us." When I reached the kitchen, the door leading to the backyard looked old, as if it had been closed for a long time. Mother appeared again in my dream and gave me the keys to open the ancient-looking kitchen door. "Open it!" Mum declared. When I opened the kitchen door, I saw a shrine (an altar) in the backyard. I screamed in anger! I found myself saying, "Who built this altar? It must be destroyed!" I was shouting in my dream; then I woke up. The dream bothered me deeply. I asked the Holy Spirit, "What is this?" The Spirit said, "Remember that it is in Ndola where your father lost everything he owned. It is also where all of you, as a family unit, got scattered into different cities. That was the beginning of your downfall!"

Ladies and gentlemen, when my dear sister Judy posted this prophetic dream on our family WhatsApp group, my spirit exploded into action. I was in America at my home in Scottsdale, Arizona. The Holy Spirit told me to come before the altar of the LORD in my home. At the time, the Spirit of God had been teaching me on the subject of altars. As soon as I knelt in prayer, the Spirit of God spoke to me. "Son, do you want to know the name of the evil altar of your father's house that you have been fighting for years?" I said, "Yes, Lord, I'm desperate for answers!"

"It's called the altar that scatters in Ndola. This is the demonic altar that has scattered many of your divine relationships, churches, businesses, open-doors, and financial opportunities that I have tried to bless you with."

I was stunned speechless. At the same time, a sense of pure relief swept over me. The mystery of my struggles in life had just been revealed. I was no longer shadowboxing a mysterious enemy.

Seizing the Horns of Destiny!

> But the Spirit of the Lord clothed Gideon with Himself and took possession of him, and he blew a trumpet, and [the clan of] Abiezer was gathered to him.
>
> (Judges 6:34)

"I want you to fly to Zambia with your wife. Take Judy and several of your blood brothers, and travel to your old house in Ndola. Go and pull down the altar of your father's house, and everything I have been trying to give you will stay with you permanently." Even though the last time I traveled to Ndola was over

28 years ago, I did not hesitate in my obedience. When my wife and I landed in Lusaka, Zambia, we rented a truck and drove with six family members to our old house in Ndola. When we arrived, I went to the backyard to the exact spot my sister was shown in her prophetic dream. We repented, prayed, and did a prophetic act of tearing down the evil altar of our father's house. We took both the idol and evil altar to the Courts of Heaven and prosecuted them.

The Spirit of God told me that it was done! The righteous judge had just handed down a righteous verdict of release and deliverance. I even asked the Lord, the righteous judge, for punitive damages against the idol and evil altar of my father's house for all the spiritual, emotional, and financial losses my family had suffered for generations. Since then, my wife and I have experienced exponential growth in our ministry in the USA and worldwide. Doors of ministry and television (closed for years) suddenly swung wide open! I was even offered a fully paid global television ministry on a major TV network!

Since we pulled down and prosecuted the evil altar of my father's house, our ministry has been flooded with donations. My personal and ministry account balances are showing figures I had only previously dreamed of having. My wife and I went from not owning any land to owning over 300 acres of farming land and a fully operational farm within six months of pulling down the evil altar and idol of my father's house! There is nothing we have done differently in the natural to merit what's taking place in our life and ministry except for the act of tearing down the evil altar of the idol of my father's house.

Let the Spirit Lead You!

For all who are allowing themselves to be led by the Spirit of God are sons of God.

(Romans 8:14)

Please remember, God is no respecter of persons. He will do the same thing for you too! It's your time! (FYI: You don't have to go to an actual physical location to tear down the altar of your father's house. That is just what the Holy Spirit required of me. You can prosecute and tear down the evil altar and idol of your father's house from the comfort of your home or office if you simply come into the Courts of heaven.) That said, a brother who heard me teach on the battle of altars in Nashville, Tennessee, heard the Holy Spirit tell him to go to his father's grave as a point of contact and tear down the altar of his father's house. He did it, and the very next day, there was a check to the tune of thousands of dollars that arrived in the mail. It had been delayed for a long time, but it was instantly released when he broke away from the evil altar of his father's house. He has been experiencing a significant increase in his life and business. The key here is to be led by the Holy Spirit!

PRAYER OF ACTIVATION!

"Heavenly Father, I ask for the Court of Heaven to be seated and for the books of my destiny to be opened as I come before the Judge of all the earth to plead my case against any evil altar in my life or bloodline that is speaking against me. I decree and declare that the Holy Spirit is my official guide and counselor in this courtroom. Heavenly Father, I surrender all rights to self-representation; instead, I ask my defense attorney and mediator of the new covenant, the Lord Jesus Christ, to represent me in your Royal Courtroom against all idols and evil altars that are controlling my life and bloodline, in any way. I also ask the Lord Jesus to heal me by His blood from all soul wounds caused by idols and evil altars in my bloodline. I am seeking a verdict of release from the power of these evil altars in Jesus' Name.

I now enter a plea of 'guilty' into the court's records concerning any legitimate accusations that Satan has filed in Court against me or my bloodline. For Jesus said, in Matthew 5:25, *"Come to terms quickly [at the earliest opportunity] with your opponent at law while you are with him on the way [to court], so that your opponent does not hand you over to the judge, and the judge to the guard, and you are thrown into prison."* Lord, since I am under oath, I cannot lie about my sinful activities and the iniquities of my bloodline that are connected to idolatry and the erecting evil altars. I repent for all sins and transgressions that I and my ancestors ever committed against you and the laws of nature. Cleanse me from all sin by the blood of Jesus, according to 1 John 1:9. I now formally submit my guilty plea and repentance to the court, in Jesus' Name."

Heavenly Father,

- I decree and declare that God has anointed and raised me as a deliverer in my family in Jesus' Name!
- I uproot and overthrow any and all evil altars of my Father's house or bloodline, in Jesus' Name!
- I decree and declare that God has given me supernatural grace to obey Him, even when I am scared, in Jesus' Name!
- I decree and declare that I bind every spiritual retaliation or push-back from the evil altar of my father's house, in Jesus' Name!
- I decree and declare that I am seizing the horns of my God-given destiny from the hands of demonic powers and evil altars, in Jesus' Name!
- I decree and declare that I am completely healed from all soul wounds that I have in common with any evil altar, in Jesus' Name!
- I decree and declare that I am a victor in the battle of altars in my life because I am led by the Holy Spirit, in Jesus' Name!

LIFE APPLICATION

SECTION

Memory Verse

That night the Lord said to Gideon, Take your father's bull, the second bull seven years old, and pull down the altar of Baal that your father has and cut down the Asherah [symbol of the goddess Asherah] that is beside it; ²⁶And build an altar to the Lord your God on top of this stronghold with stones laid in proper order. Then take the second bull and offer a burnt sacrifice with the wood of the Asherah which you shall cut down.

(Judges 6:25-26)

Reflections

1. What is the altar of your father's house?

_____

_____

_____

_____

2. What did God tell Gideon to do with the altar of his father's house?

_____

_____

_____

_____

Obeying Scared!

7

The Elijah Ministry: Rebuilding the Broken Altar of the Lord

Now Elijah the Tishbite, who was of the settlers of Gilead, said to Ahab, "As the Lord, the God of Israel lives, before whom I stand, there shall be neither dew nor rain these years, except by my word." 2And the word of the Lord came to him, saying,

(1 Kings 17:1-2)

The prophet Elijah is probably one of the most important prophetic voices in the Old Testament. He is my favorite. He arrives on the scene suddenly, seemingly out of nowhere. It is as though God was using his ministry to show us that it matters less where a person is coming from than where they're going and the impact they ultimately have when they land their destiny on a generation. That is the story of Elijah Tishbite. Elijah announced himself on the national scene by issuing a divine restraining order against the rain falling upon the nation of Israel for three years. This divine restraining order was a clear indication that Elijah commanded a place of honor and intimacy with the Lord. He was a man who knew that he was standing on a powerful altar.

Obedience: The Building of a Superior Altar

"Go from here and turn eastward and hide yourself by the brook Cherith, which is east of the Jordan [River]. ⁴You shall drink from the brook, and I have commanded the ravens to sustain you there [with food]." ⁵So he went and did in accordance with the word of the Lord; he went and lived by the brook Cherith, which is east of the Jordan. ⁶And the ravens brought him bread and meat in the morning, and bread and meat in the evening; and he would drink from the brook. ⁷It happened after a while that the brook dried up, because there was no rain in the land. ⁸Then the word of the Lord came to him, saying, ⁹"Arise, go to [a]Zarephath, which belongs to Sidon, and stay there. Behold, I have commanded a widow there to provide for you." ¹⁰So he set out and went to Zarephath, and when he came to the gate of the city, behold, a widow was there gathering sticks [for firewood].

(1 Kings 17:3-10)

One of the most important features of building an altar in the spirit world is consistency. This is because all altars are places of ritual. A ritual is a repetitive activity, so consistency is a must to build a superior altar. The Bible says in Romans 6:15, *"Do you not know that when you continually offer yourselves to someone to do his will, you are the slaves of the one whom you obey, either [slaves] of sin, which leads to death, or of obedience, which leads to righteousness (right standing with God)?"* That means that whatever we choose to yield ourselves to repeatedly is permitted to dominate our consciousness and control our actions. For instance, if a person steals once, they have a problem, but if they keep stealing consistently, soon enough, their consistency in stealing will invite a demonic spirit of stealing to join them in their habit. When this happens, an altar of stealing is born. From that moment forward, they will crave stealing with the same passion a cocaine addict longs for drugs in their system.

The same principle applies when we give ourselves over to the righteous principles of the Kingdom of God consistently. God will meet us in our consistency, and a righteous altar will be born. God knew that Elijah's primary mandate was to confront the spirit of Jezebel, which was controlling the nation of Israel and corrupting the nation with idolatry. However, the Lord knew that Elijah was not yet ready to confront Jezebel's superior evil altar, the controlling spirit over the nation. God needed to build him up in the spirit first to be the one with the superior altar. To do this, the Lord had to introduce the prophet Elijah to higher and more peculiar levels of obedience to God than he had ever experienced before. The Lord took him to the brook Cherith, where he had to believe God daily to feed him using the stingiest bird in all of creation -- the raven. From a natural standpoint, this required both faith and obedience. As the ravens consistently brought him bread and meat in the morning and evening, his faith and obedience level increased, and his altar became much more powerful. Consequently, consistent obedience to God is how we raise a superior altar.

One of the most important features of building an altar in the spirit world is consistency.

The Testing of a Superior Altar

He called out to her and said, "Please bring me a little water in a jar, so that I may drink." [11]As she was going to get it, he called to her and said, "Please bring me a piece of bread in your hand." [12]But she said, "As the Lord your God lives, I have no bread, only a handful of flour in the bowl and a little oil in the jar. See, I am gathering a few sticks so that I may go in and bake it for me and my son, that we may eat it [as our last meal] and die." [13]Elijah said to her, "Do not fear; go and do as you have said. Just make me a little bread from it first and bring it out to me, and afterward you may make one for yourself and for your son. [14]For this is what the Lord God of Israel says: 'The bowl of flour shall not be exhausted nor shall the jar of oil be empty until the day that the Lord sends rain [again] on the face of the earth.'" [15]She went and did as Elijah said. And she and he and her household ate for many days. 16

The bowl of flour was not exhausted nor did the jar of oil become empty, in accordance with the word of the Lord which He spoke through Elijah.

(1 Kings 17:10-16)

I once heard a man of God say, "God cannot trust a man whom His own hands have not formed and fashioned." That is why God will test a man or woman before He sends them out to represent His Kingdom government. It is difficult to trust what has not been tested. Consequently, the Lord, by His spirit, led the Prophet Elijah to the house of the widow who lived in a city of Sidon known as Zarepath. We need to note that Sidon (Zarepath) was Jezebel's birthplace. God took Elijah the prophet to Jezebel's backyard.

When he arrived in Zarepath he found the woman at the gate to the city, gathering a few sticks to go home and cook her last meal. She was obviously depressed because she was dreading the possibility of her and her son dying from starvation. Once again, this required tremendous faith and obedience on behalf of the prophet because the woman God had told him would take care of him, was broke and suicidal. He had to look past her immediate condition and see the miracle that she could receive under the power of the Holy Spirit. So, the first test with which the woman's situation challenged Elijah's altar was the issue or problem of provision. The woman's situation was dire, to say the least, but Elijah the prophet said to her,

"Do not fear; go and do as you have said. Just make me a little bread from it first and bring it out to me, and afterward you may make one for yourself and for your son. ¹⁴For this is what the Lord God of Israel says: 'The bowl of flour shall not be exhausted, nor shall the jar of oil be empty until the day that the Lord sends rain [again] on the face of the earth.'"

(1 Kings 17:13-14)

The prophet Elijah's superior altar, in conjunction with the power of God, made a miracle out of the woman's dire situation. The bin of flour never ran out, and the jar of oil also never ran dry. That was in the middle of a regional famine based upon the prophetic word he had released that stopped the sky above from releasing rain! Based upon this outstanding miracle of provision, that Elijah's altar was rising in spiritual stature to take on the evil altar of Jezebel, who was controlling the nation of Israel.

Elijah Raises the Widow's Son in Jezebel's Territory

> It happened after these things, that the son of the woman, the mistress of the house, became sick; and his illness was so severe that there was no breath left in him.

> So she said to Elijah, "What [problem] is there between you and me, O man of God? Have you come to me to bring my sin to mind and to put my son to death?" ¹⁹He said to her, "Give me your son." Then he took him from her arms and carried him up to the upper room where he was living, and laid him on his own bed. ²⁰He called to the Lord and said, "O Lord my God, have You brought further tragedy to the widow with whom I am staying, by causing her son to die?" ²¹Then he stretched himself out upon the child three times, and called to the Lord and said, "O Lord my God, please let this child's life return to him." ²²The Lord heard the voice of Elijah, and the life of the child returned to him and he revived. ²³Elijah took the child and brought him down from the upper room into the [lower part of the] house and gave him to his mother; and Elijah said, "See, your son is alive." ²⁴Then the woman said to Elijah, "Now I know that you are a man of God and that the word of the Lord in your mouth is truth."
>
> (1 Kings 17:17-24)

While Elijah, the prophet, was staying at the widow woman's house, something tragic happened. But I believe the Lord allowed it to increase his stature in the spirit and strengthen Elijah's altar. The widow's son died. Like any caring mother, the widow panicked, and this is what she said to the Prophet, *"What [problem] is there between you and me, O man of God? Have you come to me to bring my sin to mind and to put my son to death?"* To Elijah's credit, he did not panic. He simply said, "Give me your son." Then he took him from her arms and carried him up to the upper room where he was living and laid him on his bed. He called to the Lord and said,

> *"O Lord my God, have You brought further tragedy to the widow with whom I am staying, by causing her son to die?" Then he stretched himself out upon the child three times, and called to the Lord and said, "O Lord my God, please let this child's life return to him." The Lord heard the voice of Elijah, and the life of the child returned to him and he revived. Elijah took the child and brought him down from the upper room into the [lower part of the] house and gave him to his mother; and Elijah said, "See, your son is alive." Then the woman said to Elijah, "Now I know that you are a man of God and that the word of the Lord in your mouth is truth."*

Do you understand the significance of what just happened here? Elijah, the prophet, had just resurrected a child in Jezebel's backyard! Please remember that this miracle of resurrection happened in Sidon, which was Jezebel's birthplace. That is where she grew up and where she started watching Baal and the Asherah build altars to these demonic gods. 1 Kings 16:31 says this, *"It came about, as if it had been a trivial thing for Ahab to walk in the sins of Jeroboam the son of Nebat, that he married Jezebel the daughter of Ethbaal king of the Sidonians, and went and served Baal and worshiped him."* The City of Sidon was full of altars to Jezebel's deities, and these demonic gods failed to stop Elijah from overcoming the spirit of death in their backyard! Talk about taking the fight to the enemy! That was it! God had just made this point to Elijah and convinced him beyond any reasonable doubt that his altar had become more powerful than Jezebel's altar. Now he was ready to confront the national spirit that was corrupting the nation of Israel and its human attendant -- Jezebel!

An Apostolic Commissioning

Now it happened after many days that the word of the Lord came to Elijah in the third year, saying, "Go, show yourself to Ahab, and I will send rain on the face of the earth." ²So Elijah went to show himself to Ahab. Now the famine was severe in Samaria.

(1 Kings 18:1-2)

Immediately after, the Lord called the prophet Elijah out of exile. He told him to go back to Israel and confront the worship of Baal and its network of evil altars that Jezebel had planted all over the nation. In other words, the prophet Elijah was now ready for the most intensive battle of altars his ministry had ever experienced. This is the essence of the Elijah story: it's about the battle of altars. It's about the confrontation in the spirit world between the righteous altar of Elijah representing God's Kingdom and a myriad of evil altars spread across the nation of Israel under Jezebel's evil influence. In essence, when the Bible promises to return the spirit of Elijah to us, it is truly a loaded promise. The implication is that when the spirit of Elijah is restored to the Church, the Body of Christ will acquire spiritual stature in the spirit world to confront evil, national altars that are corrupting nations.

God or Baal: The Battle of Altars?

Now then, send word and gather to me all Israel at Mount Carmel, together with the 450 prophets of Baal and the 400 prophets of [the goddess] Asherah, who eat at [Queen] Jezebel's table." ²⁰So Ahab sent word to all the Israelites and assembled the [pagan] prophets together at Mount Carmel. ²¹Elijah approached all the people and said, "How long will you [c]hesitate between two opinions? If the Lord is God, follow Him; but if Baal, follow him." But the people [of Israel] did not answer him [so much as] a word. ²²Then Elijah said to the people, "I alone remain a prophet of the Lord, while Baal's prophets are 450 men. ²³Now let them give us two oxen, and let them choose one ox for themselves and cut it in pieces, and lay it on the wood, but put no

128

fire under it. I will prepare the other ox and lay it on the wood, and I will not put a fire under it. ²⁴Then you call on the name of your god, and I will call on the name of the Lord; and the god who answers by fire, He is God." And all the people answered, "It is well spoken."

(1 Kings 18:19-24)

As soon as the prophet Elijah arrived from his divinely imposed exile, the spiritual atmosphere in Israel shifted. The battle of altars was on! He appeared to a disciple by the name of Obadiah, who had been taking care of 100 prophets of God in secret caves to save their necks from Jezebel's wrath. He told him to call King Ahab, who came immediately, and when he saw Elijah, he began to accuse him for all of Israel's troubles. But Elijah responded that he was not the troublemaker of Israel. It was he and Jezebel who were troubling Israel by corrupting it with idolatry. Elijah then told the king to call the 450 prophets of Baal and the 400 prophets of the goddess Asherah who ate at Jezebel's table to come and meet him at Mount Carmel for the ultimate battle of altars.

On Mount Carmel, the prophet Elijah rebuked the people of Israel for wavering in between two opinions. He told them that if Baal is God, then serve him. However, if the Lord, the God of Israel, was their true God, then they needed to serve Him and abandon these worthless idols. Then he offered the people a challenge that was supernatural in nature; they could not resist. Here is what he said. *"I alone remain a prophet of the Lord, while Baal's prophets are 450 men. Now let them give us two oxen and let them choose one ox for themselves and cut it in pieces, and lay it on the wood, but put no fire under it. I will prepare the other ox and lay it on the wood, and I will not put a fire under it. Then you call on the name of your god, and I will call on the name of the Lord; and the god who answers by fire, He is God." And all the people answered, "It is well spoken."* As soon as the people responded, "It is well spoken," the battle of altars on Mount Carmel, was on!

Repairing the Broken Altar of the Lord

Then Elijah said to all the people, "Come near to me." So, all the people approached him. And he repaired and rebuilt the [old] altar of the Lord that had been torn down [by Jezebel]. ³¹Then Elijah took twelve stones in accordance with the number of the tribes of the sons of Jacob, to whom the word of the Lord had come, saying, "Israel shall be your name." ³²So with the stones Elijah built an altar in the name of the Lord.

(1 Kings 18:30-32)

What soon followed Elijah's challenge was the greatest spectacle in futility ever recorded in Scripture. It demonstrated the futility of worshiping idols and erecting evil altars. The 850 prophets of Baal and the goddess Asherah built an altar and placed a bull on it. They chanted all day long as they begged these Phoenician deities to release supernatural fire that would consume the sacrifice. But after hours of incantations and endless chanting, nothing came of it. After a while, the prophet Elijah began to mock them in front of the people. He told them to cry out louder because maybe their deities were asleep and needed to be awakened. He was genuinely having fun, demonstrating the complete superiority of the God of Israel and the strength of his personal altar.

After it was abundantly clear to everyone watching the 850 prophets of Baal and the goddess Asherah that they had come up empty, Elijah finally took his turn. And this is what he did and said: *"Come near to me." So, all the people approached him. And he repaired and rebuilt the [old] altar of the Lord that had been torn down [by Jezebel]. Then Elijah took twelve stones in accordance with the number of the tribes of the sons of Jacob, to whom the word of the Lord had come, saying, "Israel shall be your name." So, with the stones Elijah built an altar in the name of the Lord."* I will never forget the first time I had heard my dear friend Tony Kemp who was taken to heaven by the Lord. While he was in heaven, he was given a chance to meet with Elijah. Elijah told him something that triggered my interest in the subject of altars.

Even before I heard what Tony Kemp would tell me, the prophet Elijah was my favorite Old Testament prophet. I used his story a lot in my teachings.

130

My favorite teaching was titled "The God Who Answers By Fire," which is a direct quote from Elijah's encounter with the prophets of Baal on Mount Carmel. For the longest time, I saw Elijah's ministry as a ministry of releasing the fire of God. However, this is not how Elijah described the essence of his ministry when Tony met him in heaven. Here is what Elijah told Tony, "Many people think my ministry is about releasing the fire, but my ministry was about the repairing of the broken altar of the Lord in a generation." When I heard this, I was blown away. It suddenly dawned on me that the "fire of God" that fell from heaven only happened after Elijah repaired and restored the broken altar of the Lord.

The God who Answers by Fire!

At the time of the offering of the evening sacrifice, Elijah the prophet approached [the altar] and said, "O Lord, the God of Abraham, Isaac, and Israel (Jacob), let it be known today that You are God in Israel and that I am Your servant and that I have done all these things at Your word. ³⁷Answer me, O Lord, answer me, so that this people may know that You, O Lord, are God, and that You have turned their hearts back [to You]." ³⁸Then the fire of the Lord fell and consumed the burnt offering and the wood, and even the stones and the dust; it also licked up the water in the trench. ³⁹When all the people saw it, they fell face downward; and they said, "The Lord, He is God! The Lord, He is God!"

(1 Kings 18:36-39)

After Elijah repaired the broken altar of the Lord and cried to the Lord to redeem His people, the fire of God fell from heaven. It consumed the sacrificial bull and all the water that Elijah had poured over the altar. When the people saw the supernatural fire of God that fell from heaven, their hearts shifted, and they began to bow in worship, as they cried, "The Lord, He is God! The Lord, He is God!" The moral of this story is that when we repair the broken altar of the Lord or raise an altar to the Lord, God's supernatural fire will overshadow us. Miracles, signs, and wonders in the Kingdom don't happen in a vacuum: they demand that those who perform miracles are connected to an altar. Even witches or sorcerers who perform lying signs and wonders are standing on an altar. No one can escape passing through an altar if they desire supernatural power.

༄ ༄ ༄ ༄

Elijah's ministry was about the repairing of the broken altar of the Lord in a generation.

༄ ༄ ༄ ༄

The Sound of an Abundance of Rain!

Now Elijah said to Ahab, "Go up, eat and drink, for there is the sound of the roar of an abundance of rain." 42 So Ahab went up to eat and to drink. And Elijah went up to the top of Carmel; and he crouched down to the earth and put his face between his knees, 43 and he said to his servant, "Go up, look toward the sea." So, he went up and looked and said, "There is nothing." Elijah said, "Go back" seven times. 44 And at the seventh time the servant said, "A cloud as small as a man's hand is coming up from the sea."

(1 Kings 18:41-44)

Elijah's repairing of the altar of the Lord precipitated the release of a "sound of an abundance of rain." Remember, the land had been under divine judgment, so a famine was ruling the territory. As soon as the ruling principality, Baal, had been toppled, the judgment of God was removed. Before the rain came, God sent a sound, the "sound of an abundance of rain." Evil altars in your bloodline have stolen monies and inheritances that God ordained for you to enjoy. As you repair the broken altar of the Lord in your life, get ready for God to release the spirit of abundance in your life, like never before!

The Spirit of Acceleration!

And Elijah said, "Go up, say to Ahab, 'Prepare your chariot and go down, so that the rain shower does not stop you.'" [45] In a little while the sky grew dark with clouds and wind, and there were heavy showers. And Ahab mounted and rode [his chariot] and went [inland] to Jezreel. [46] Then the hand of the Lord came upon Elijah [giving him supernatural strength]. He girded up his loins and outran Ahab to the entrance of Jezreel [nearly twenty miles].

(1 Kings 18:44-46)

One of the most important things that came out of Elijah's actions on Mount Carmel is the release of the spirit of acceleration. He told King Ahab that rain was coming. The skies quickly became dark and pregnant with rain. He told Ahab that the rain would come so fast, if he didn't get into his chariots and ride to Jezreel, the rainstorm would overtake him. Soon after, the rains began to fall. The hand of the Lord came upon the prophet, and Elijah outran a chariot of horses into town. How incredible is this? The underlying principle here is that when we are standing on a superior altar, we can outrun any demonic or natural strategy designed to stop or delay our progress! We can outperform any competition. This is why we need to understand the spiritual ramifications of the "Battle of Altars!"

PRAYER OF ACTIVATION!

"Heavenly Father, I ask for the Court of Heaven to be seated and for the books of my destiny to be opened as I come before the Judge of all the earth to plead my case against any evil altar in my life or bloodline that is speaking against me. I decree and declare that the Holy Spirit is my official guide and counselor in this courtroom. Heavenly Father, I surrender all rights to self-representation; instead, I ask my defense attorney and mediator of the new covenant, the Lord Jesus Christ, to represent me in your Royal Courtroom against all idols and evil altars that are controlling my life and bloodline, in any way. I also ask the Lord Jesus to heal me by His blood from all soul wounds caused by idols and evil altars in my bloodline. I am seeking a verdict of release from the power of these evil altars in Jesus' Name.

I now enter a plea of 'guilty' into the court's records concerning any legitimate accusations that Satan has filed in Court against me or my bloodline. For Jesus said, in Matthew 5:25, *"Come to terms quickly [at the earliest opportunity] with your opponent at law while you are with him on the way [to court], so that your opponent does not hand you over to the judge, and the judge to the guard, and you are thrown into prison."* Lord, since I am under oath, I cannot lie about my sinful activities and the iniquities of my bloodline that are connected to idolatry and the erecting evil altars. I repent for all sins and transgressions that I and my ancestors ever committed against you and the laws of nature. Cleanse me from all sin by the blood of Jesus, according to 1 John 1:9. I now formally submit my guilty plea and repentance to the court, in Jesus' name."

Heavenly Father,

- I decree and declare that each time I obey the Holy Spirit or the word of God, I am building a superior altar that can speak for me in the Courts of Heaven, in Jesus' Name!
- I decree and declare that I have God-given spiritual authority to raise the dead in Jezebel's backyard, in Jesus' Name!
- I decree and declare that all opposing and evil altars against me are destroyed in Jesus' Name!
- I decree and declare that God has supernaturally commissioned me to be a destroyer of evil altars in my bloodline, in Jesus' Name!
- I decree and declare that Baal's evil altar is completely destroyed in my life, in Jesus' Name!
- I decree and declare that I am completely healed from all soul wounds, which Satan was using against me, in Jesus' Name!
- I decree and declare that I carry the revelation of the God who answers by fire, in Jesus' Name!

LIFE APPLICATION

SECTION

Memory Verse

Then Elijah said to all the people, "Come near to me." So, all the people approached him. And he repaired and rebuilt the [old] altar of the Lord that had been torn down [by Jezebel]. 31Then Elijah took twelve stones in accordance with the number of the tribes of the sons of Jacob, to whom the word of the Lord had come, saying, "Israel shall be your name." 32So with the stones Elijah built an altar in the name of the Lord.

(1 Kings 18:30-32)

Reflections

1. Why is obedience so important in the process of building a superior altar?

   _____

   _____

   _____

   _____

2. How did God show Elijah that he had a superior altar to Jezebel's evil altars?

   _____

   _____

   _____

   _____

8

Erecting an Altar in Your Home & Business

"Also, when you pray, do not be like the hypocrites; for they love to pray [publicly] standing in the synagogues and on the corners of the streets so that they may be seen by men. I assure you and most solemnly say to you, they [already] have their reward in full.

(Matthew 6:5)

---

rom Genesis to Revelation, the Bible presents God as being both personal and corporate, one who desires a sincere and intimate relationship with His creation. Since God desires a sincere relationship with His children, He hates hypocrisy and duplicity in those who come near Him. In the above passage of Scripture, Jesus deals with the issue of hypocrisy head-on as it relates to the realm of prayer and shows us how dangerous it is. Jesus rebukes the Pharisees and Sadducees for bringing the spirit of showmanship to the realm and altar of prayer. We have already mentioned how prayer is one of the most important altar activities, so building our personal altar of prayer is very important to God.

Erect Your Home Altar: in Your Most Private Room

But when you pray, go into your most private room, close the door and pray to your Father who is in secret, and your Father who sees [what is done] in secret will reward you.

(Matthew 6:6)

Because having a personal altar of prayer is very important to God, Jesus went out of His way to show us the best location to position our personal altar of prayer in our home. It is in our most private room. First and foremost, the expression "your most private room" (or prayer closet) eliminates the spirit of showmanship. Our personal altar of prayer must retain a sense of secrecy and intimacy in how this altar is structured. Our home altar is supposed to be a bastion of intimacy between the living God and us. This means that our private room of prayer must be protected from the noise and ranker of our daily home chores. Ever since the Lord gave my wife and me the revelation of the importance of an altar in our home, we have endeavored to build a personal altar of prayer in a special room in our house dedicated to this special purpose. I am aware that some people may not have an extra room in their house to dedicate for this special purpose. I suggest that you put up a small tent in a special corner of your house that will be dedicated to the Lord to function as your personal altar of prayer.

Second, the expression, "your most private room," conveys the picture of the marriage bed-chamber. Typically, the marriage bed chamber is reserved for the husband and wife as a place of intimacy that the public cannot access. That is why a sexual scandal breaks out when the public discovers that a couple invited a third eye in their sexual union. Recently the evangelical world in America was rocked by a sexual scandal of one of its top Christian leaders who was the president of a famous Christian university. It was discovered that he and his wife were entangled in a three-some sexual affair with a much younger man for over eight years. This sexual scandal caused this well-known Christian leader to resign his post as the president of this university. Both the secular world and the Christian church were rightfully appalled by this well-known

Christian couple's scandalous behavior. Everybody knew they had violated the sanctity of the marriage bed. Jesus was conveying the idea of the sanctity and secrecy of the marriage bed when He was teaching us how to build a personal altar of prayer in our home.

Building Intimacy with God on Your Home Altar

"And when you pray, do not use meaningless repetition as the Gentiles do, for they think they will be heard because of their many words. 8So do not be like them [praying as they do]; for your Father knows what you need before you ask Him.

(Matthew 6:7)

Since building a personal altar of prayer in our home is about building intimacy with God, Jesus warned us against using it as a place for meaningless repetitions of meaningless prayers before God. Our personal altar of prayer is not supposed to be a place for impressing our spirituality on God or others. First and foremost, we cannot impress God, anyway! There is nothing about us that the Lord doesn't already know. However, God sincerely desires an intimate and dynamic relationship with us. After all, we are His beloved children. He sent Jesus to die for us on the cross for the very purpose of restoring our lost relationship of intimacy.

When Adam and Eve lost the crown of glory and intimacy after listening to the serpent and disobeying God by eating the forbidden tree, God still came after them in the cool of the day, longing to restore the broken relationship fellowship. Here is how the Bible records God's passionate pursuit of fallen man in the Garden of Eden. In Genesis 3:7 it says, *"And they heard the sound of the LORD God walking in the garden in the cool [afternoon breeze] of the day, so the man and his wife hid and kept themselves hidden from the [a] presence of the LORD God among the trees of the garden. But the LORD God called to Adam, and said to him, "Where are you?"* This Scripture passage makes me teary-eyed because it paints a picture of a God who will never stop pursuing me even when I stink with sin! Hallelujah!

When Jesus says, *"So do not be like them [praying as they do]; for your Father knows what you need before you ask Him."* He completely transformed our home altar of prayer from being an engine of meaningless religious activity to a spiritual platform for establishing an authentic and meaningful intimate relationship with the God who created us. Jesus clarifies that our altar of prayer is not about asking God to meet the laundry list of our daily needs. Our heavenly Father already knows whatever we need, even before we asked for it! That being the case, our altar of prayer is more about knowing God intimately than manipulating God to meet our needs. However, it's apparent and definitely implied that the more we spend time with God, the more he will meet our personal needs. Glory to God!

Our personal altar of prayer must retain a sense of secrecy and intimacy around it in terms of how this altar is structured.

Experiencing the Kingdom Through Your Home Altar

"Pray, then, in this way: 'Our Father, who is in heaven, Hallowed be Your name. [10]'Your kingdom come, Your will be done on earth as it is in heaven. [11]'Give us this day our daily bread .[12]'And forgive us our debts, as we have forgiven our debtors [letting go of both the wrong and the resentment].[13]'And do not lead us into temptation, but deliver us from evil. [For Yours is the kingdom and the power and the glory forever. Amen.]'

(Matthew 6:9-13)

After Jesus finished establishing the nature and spiritual dynamic of the kind of personal altar of prayer, He wants us to build for Him in our homes; He then moves on to establish "how we ought to pray!" How we are to pray would then establish the spiritual experience we can expect from a properly functioning personal altar of prayer. Jesus said, *"Pray, then, in this way: 'Our*

Father, who is in heaven." So, from our altar of prayer in our home, we are supposed to come to know Him as our heavenly Father. It is in spending time with God daily that we come into the understanding that even though our earthly fathers may abandon us, we have a Father in heaven who will never leave nor forsake us.

Jesus goes on to say, *"Hallowed be Your name."* This expression, "Hallowed be your name," means that it is from our personal altar of prayer that we come to terms with just how holy God is. His name is exalted in all the earth. We will find ourselves engrossed in realms of worship as we have never known before. When Jesus goes on to say, *"Your kingdom come, Your will be done on earth as it is in heaven,"* He lets us know that we are supposed to come into a real Kingdom experience from meeting with God on our altar of prayer. There was no message Jesus preached on earth that was more important to Him than the Gospel of the Kingdom. Whenever Jesus had an opportunity to teach or preach, He spoke on the Gospel of the Kingdom. So, it is not surprising that Jesus is teaching us in the above passage of Scripture that when we spend time with God in our secret room of prayer, the Holy Spirit will bring us into a real Kingdom experience.

Jesus goes on to show us that once we begin to experience the Kingdom, God's will for us will be done here on earth as it is in heaven. He even shows us that our daily needs for provision and sustenance will be met in our secret place of prayer. Even the spiritual debts we owe to the Lord will be wiped out. From our home altar of prayer, God wants to teach us how to forgive others who have previously offended us. At our prayer altar is where we learn the spiritual discipline of living in forgiveness. From spending time with God in this place of intimacy, we will learn how to hear His voice and thus avoid falling into the temptations the devil throws our way.

Killing the Spirit of Unforgiveness on Your Home Altar

For if you forgive others their trespasses [their reckless and willful sins], your heavenly Father will also forgive you. ¹⁵But if you do not forgive others [nurturing your hurt and anger with the result that it interferes with your relationship with God], then your Father will not forgive your trespasses.

(Matthew 6:14-15)

After many years of walking with the Lord and meeting people around the world, I have discovered that there is nothing that stops believers from growing in Christ more than the spirit of unforgiveness. I am convinced that the spirit of unforgiveness is the number one spiritual cancer that is destroying the Body of Christ. However, in the above passage of Scripture, the Lord Jesus Christ connects our ability to overcome the spirit of unforgiveness with having a functional personal altar of prayer with God. I love the Amplified version of the above passage of Scripture because it shows us that harboring unforgiveness is like nurturing our anger and hurt with the result that they interfere with our relationship with God. That is why God wants to empower us in our personal time of prayer and fellowship so that we rise in spiritual stature above the tentacles of the spirit of unforgiveness. Glory to His holy name!

I cannot tell you the number of times I was spending time with God on my altar of prayer when the Spirit of God brought up the memory of someone I had not yet forgiven. I knew instinctively, and by the Spirit, that if I did not forgive the person, the Holy Spirit was showing me, my time with God would be severely compromised. I don't know about you, but in such moments the Holy Spirit refuses to give me peace and the passion to continue pursuing His presence until I deal with the issue of unforgiveness in my heart, truthfully and permanently. The spirit of unforgiveness is also the reason many marriages are ending in divorce. Couples cannot seem to get past the last offense, so they harbor unforgiveness until it poisons and destroys their marriage. I am convinced that if most couples had built a personal home altar of prayer, the Lord would have used their "home altar of prayer" to rescue their marriages from ending up in the divorce court.

Fasting on Your Home Altar

> *"And whenever you are fasting, do not look gloomy like the hypocrites, for they put on a sad and dismal face [like actors, discoloring their faces with ashes or dirt] so that their fasting may be seen by men. I assure you and most solemnly say to you, they [already] have their reward in full. [17]But when you fast, put oil on your head [as you normally would to groom your hair] and wash your face [18]so that your fasting will not be noticed by people, but by your Father who is in secret; and your Father who sees [what is done] in secret will reward you.*
>
> (Matthew 6:16-18)

One of the most important spiritual activities a child of God can ever be engaged in is the spiritual discipline of fasting. Jesus fasted, and He also prayed fervently. The Bible combines these two spiritual disciplines. They are twin disciplines. Since prayer and fasting are essential rituals around an altar, Jesus went out of His way to explain how we ought to fast and how to behave during a fast. This is the warning Jesus gave us about fasting, *"Whenever you are fasting, do not look gloomy like the hypocrites, for they put on a sad and dismal face [like actors, discoloring their faces with ashes or dirt] so that their fasting may be seen by men. I assure you and most solemnly say to you, they [already] have their reward in full."* In other words, if we look gloomy and sanctimonious when we are fasting, all the benefits that would have accrued to our personal altar of prayer will be wasted. Instead of increasing in spiritual stature, our home altar of prayer will be significantly diminished.

Thankfully, Jesus did not stop at warning us against how not to fast. He also went on to show us how to fast. This is what Jesus said about how to fast: *"But when you fast, put oil on your head [as you normally would to groom your hair] and wash your face, so that your fasting will not be noticed by people, but by your Father who is in secret; and your Father who sees [what is done] in secret will reward you."*

Since Jesus taught us how to fast from the perspective of having a personal "secret room of prayer," He maintains the argument that even when God impresses upon our hearts to fast, we must do it from the "marriage bed chamber" mentality. Like prayer and fellowship before it, fasting from our secret room of prayer requires an attitude of worshipful secrecy.

The Home Altar Pays the House Bills!

But when you pray, go into your most private room, close the door and pray to your Father who is in secret, and your Father who sees [what is don e] in secret will reward you.

(Matthew 6:6)

One of the most important revelations the Lord has ever given me on the subject of altars is that "the home altar pays the house bills!" I want you to meditate on this statement deeply and prayerfully because this can change your life. There's nothing that stresses people, especially married couples, more than unpaid house bills. Unpaid house bills are a threat to your livelihood because, at any moment, your lights could be cut off due to an unpaid electric bill. This is incredibly stressful when you have little children in the home. Some of you reading this book have had the unfortunate experience of being put out of your home because you were delinquent on the mortgage. Consequently, your house was repossessed by the bank.

I remember it like it happened yesterday, how the Lord gave me the revelation that the home altar pays the house bills. My wife and I had been living in a costly apartment in Scottsdale, Arizona. It was one of those very exclusive and upscale apartment buildings. When our lease was up, we decided to look for a different and less expensive apartment. My wife, who is very gifted at research, found us a lovely apartment nearby, which was $1000 less than what we were currently paying. We were so excited! So, we made an appointment to go and look at the apartment.

The apartment manager took us for a tour of the studio apartment we were trying to rent. We liked it very much. We promised to return to finalize the new lease. However, on our way home, I sensed that the Holy Spirit was grieved with our decision. I was disturbed by this, so I inquired of the Lord why He was displeased with our decision. This is what He said to me. "So, you will move into an apartment which does not have a special room that you can dedicate as an altar to Me, to save $1000? The apartment you are currently living in has a special room dedicated as an altar to Me. Do you mean to tell Me that I would not pay you an extra thousand dollars a month to protect My altar? Francis, how valuable is My altar to you?"

I was stunned speechless. I had not even considered that our desire to downsize and save money was an insult to God. Needless to say, that was the end of our search for a new apartment. My wife and I repented to the Lord for not consulting Him before we started looking for a much cheaper apartment. We extended our lease and stayed in the more expensive apartment because we finally saw the value of the "special room" that we had dedicated as an altar to the Lord. God did not disappoint. He went out of His way to provide for us financially on a level that has only grown larger every year since. We never missed a rent payment. As a matter of fact, all our house bills were paid on time. Our apartment rental, in many cases, was paid two to three months in advance. Since then, I have advised couples and singles alike that if you want to pay your house bills, build God an altar in your home. It's no wonder Obed-edom in the Old Testament was mightily blessed within three months after he hosted the Ark of God in his home after King David left it in his care. Here is what the Bible says about this amazing event:

> *David was unwilling to move the ark of the LORD into the City of David with him; instead he took it aside to the house of Obed-edom the Gittite. [11]So the ark of the LORD remained in the house of Obed-edom the Gittite for three months, and the LORD blessed Obed-edom and all his household (family). [12]Now King David was told, "The LORD has blessed the house of Obed-edom and all that belongs to him, because of the ark of God." So*

David went and brought up the ark of God from the house of Obed-edom into the City of David with rejoicing and gladness.

(2 Samuel 6:10-12)

Building an Altar in Your Business!

Abram passed through the land as far as the site of Shechem, to the [great] terebinth (oak) tree of Moreh. Now the Canaanites were in the land at that time. ⁷Then the Lord appeared to Abram and said, "I will give this land to your descendants." So Abram built an altar there to [honor] the Lord who had appeared to him.

(Genesis 12:6-7)

In closing, I want to discuss the importance of building an altar to the Lord in your place of business. Whatever you think of Buddhists, they have no qualms about openly erecting altars to Buddha in their places of business. When is the last time you patronized a Thai restaurant or a Thai massage place? Did you quickly notice that these places of business have an image and altar to Buddha in plain sight of customers? My wife is of Asian descent, so she loves Thai restaurants. They serve foods she grew up eating. However, every time we are there, we pray fervently over our food. The message is unambiguous; the Buddhist owners of these restaurants are fully dedicated to the altar of Buddha and see this false god as an integral part of their business.

Unfortunately, so many Christians who love Jesus don't have an altar in their place of business dedicated to the Lord Jesus Christ. It's no wonder we are losing the battle of altars in the marketplace. Thankfully, our father Abraham and many of the patriarchs in the Bible were not afraid or ashamed of building an altar to God in the marketplace. In the agricultural economy that they lived in, the land was their place of business. The first thing Abraham did when he arrived in the land of promise, which served as his place of business, so to speak, is raise an altar to the Lord. This altar became a place of divine encounter within his marketplace career. I am not suggesting that you place a giant statue of Jesus in front of your business, but I am suggesting that you dedicate one of the offices in your place of business as an altar to the Lord and then watch how God blesses your business!

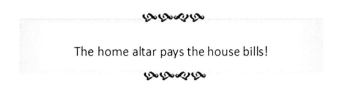

The home altar pays the house bills!

PRAYER OF ACTIVATION!

"Heavenly Father, I ask for the Court of Heaven to be seated and for the books of my destiny to be opened as I come before the Judge of all the earth to plead my case against any evil altar in my life or bloodline that is speaking against me. I decree and declare that the Holy Spirit is my official guide and counselor in this courtroom. Heavenly Father, I surrender all rights to self-representation; instead, I ask my defense attorney and mediator of the new covenant, the Lord Jesus Christ, to represent me in your Royal Courtroom against all idols and evil altars that are controlling my life and bloodline, in any way. I also ask the Lord Jesus to heal me by His blood from all soul wounds caused by idols and evil altars in my bloodline. I am seeking a verdict of release from the power of these evil altars in Jesus' Name.

I now enter a plea of 'guilty' into the court's records concerning any legitimate accusations that Satan has filed in Court against me or my bloodline. For Jesus said, in Matthew 5:25, "*Come to terms quickly [at the earliest opportunity] with your opponent at law while you are with him on the way [to court], so that your opponent does not hand you over to the judge, and the judge to the guard, and you are thrown into prison.*" Lord, since I am under oath, I cannot lie about my sinful activities and the iniquities of my bloodline that are connected to idolatry and the erecting evil altars. I repent for all sins and transgressions that I and my ancestors ever committed against you and the laws of nature. Cleanse me from all sin by the blood of Jesus, according to 1 John 1:9. I now formally submit my guilty plea and repentance to the court, in Jesus' Name."

Heavenly Father,

- I decree and declare that Satan will not stop me from erecting and consecrating an altar to the Lord in my home, in Jesus' Name!
- I decree and declare that the evil altar of slumber in my life or bloodline is completely destroyed, in Jesus' Name!
- I decree and declare that I am building an altar of intimacy with God in my home, in Jesus' Name!
- I decree and declare that I release the power of God's Kingdom in my life by erecting a righteous stationary altar in my home, in Jesus' Name!
- I decree and declare that God is setting me free from the evil altar of unforgiveness, in Jesus' Name!
- I decree and declare that I am completely healed from all soul wounds, which have kept me from erecting an altar to the Lord in my home, in Jesus' Name!
- I decree and declare that every time I go on a fast, my home altar will become stronger and stronger, in Jesus' Name!

LIFE APPLICATION

SECTION

Memory Verse

"Also, when you pray, do not be like the hypocrites; for they love to pray [publicly] standing in the synagogues and on the corners of the streets so that they may be seen by men. I assure you and most solemnly say to you, they [already] have their reward in full.

(Matthew 6:5)

Reflections

1. What is the importance of having a consecrated stationary altar in your home?

_____

_____

_____

_____

2. Why did Jesus suggest we build our home altar in our most private room?

_____

_____

_____

_____

9

Funeral Altars

For we know that if the earthly tent [our physical body] which is our house is torn down [through death], we have a building from God, a house not made with hands, eternal in the heavens. [2]For indeed in this house we groan, longing to be clothed with our [immortal, eternal] celestial dwelling, [3]so that by putting it on we will not be found naked. [4]For while we are in this tent, we groan, being burdened [often weighed down, oppressed], not that we want to be unclothed [separated by death from the body], but to be clothed, so that what is mortal [the body] will be swallowed up by life [after the resurrection].

(2 Corinthians 5:1-4)

---

*P*erhaps nothing has captured the collective consciousness of people like our common fear of death. Death is the one inescapable fate all humans share equally regardless of race or social status. Whether we are rich or poor, one thing we know for sure is that we are going to die, and so are those we love dearly. Thankfully, no book in world history deals with the subject of death as eloquently as the Bible. In making its point, the Bible makes it clear that this physical body of ours is nothing but an earthly tent that will eventually be torn down through death. Thankfully, we have a building from God – our regenerated spirit man that is already joined to the Lord in heavenly places.

Saint Paul makes it clear that the cry for immortality is built into our physical bodies of dirt, and this voice is highly amplified once a person comes into the saving knowledge of Jesus Christ. Every child of God groans inwardly with a deep-seated desire to put off mortality and put on the mantle of immortality. However, this does not mean that dying or losing a loved one is easy. As one who has experienced the death of two parents within 12 months of each other, I can tell you that going through this valley of the shadow of death was both painful and exciting at the same time. It was exciting because both of my parents were radically saved. They both loved Jesus very much, and I knew without a shadow of a doubt that heaven was their destination. However, losing two parents is no child's play. It's painful and sad. There are days I feel fine, and then there are days I cannot stop crying because I miss them a lot. I'm sure many of you can relate.

Don't Chain Yourself to a Funeral Altar!

Now we do not want you to be uninformed, believers, about those who are asleep [in death], so that you will not grieve [for them] as the others do who have no hope [beyond this present life]. [14]*For if we believe that Jesus died and rose again [as in fact He did], even so God [in this same way—by raising them from the dead] will bring with Him those [believers] who have fallen asleep in Jesus.* [15]*For we say this to you by the Lord's [own] word, that we who are still alive and remain until the coming of the Lord, will in no way precede [into His presence] those [believers] who have fallen asleep [in death].*

(1 Thessalonians 4:13-15)

Whereas celebrating the home-going of our loved ones and honoring the life they lived on earth is needful, we must be careful that we do not bind our soul to a funeral altar by mourning for them in a manner that displeases the Lord. Mourning, which does not consider the resurrection of the righteous dead, is mourning that does not please the Lord. That is why Apostle Paul admonishes New Testament believers not to mourn as though they are a people without what the Bible calls the "blessed hope." It's important to note that in the book of First Thessalonians, the Apostle Paul uses the metaphor of going to sleep for men and women who died in the Lord. If that's the case, how we mourn the righteous dead is significant to God and reveals how conscious we are of our heavenly home that Jesus purchased for us with His blood.

I will never forget when the Holy Spirit told me about the "funeral altar" and how it operates. He showed me that when the coffin of a dead person is brought into the house of God and placed at the altar (pulpit), a funeral altar is immediately created. The pastor or priest officiating the funeral ceremony becomes the human attendant to the altar. If a person inside the coffin was not a born-again believer, standing next to this funeral altar can be dangerous, spiritually speaking, if we are not covered by the blood of Jesus. Most importantly, if we have things in our soul in-common with the deceased, any demonic spirits which were residing in the body of the deceased can easily transfer their residency into spiritually vulnerable people gathered around the funeral altar. This is why Jesus said this in John 14:30, *"I will not speak with you much longer, for the ruler of the world (Satan) is coming. And he has no claim on Me [no power over Me nor anything that he can use against Me."* The implication of this verse is obvious: if we have anything in common with the ruler of this world, Satan can exercise legal claim on us. In such cases, Satan will retain his power over us. This is why we must ask the Holy Spirit to heal us of every wound in our soul that gives Satan the legal right to steal, kill, and destroy.

Even before the Lord gave me the revelation on the battle of altars, I have seen some strange things happen at funerals I have attended in Africa and the United States of America. I have seen people get into a fight at a funeral as to who would speak the deceased person's eulogy. I have seen loved ones hug their deceased coffin and demand that the deceased person take them with them. Many of these people were utterly inconsolable. It was evident that they possessed zero faith in the promised resurrection of the dead, which is one of the most important doctrines of the Church.

Now if Christ is preached as raised from the dead, how is it that some among you say that there is no resurrection of the dead? [13]But if there is no resurrection of the dead, then not even Christ has been raised; ¹⁴and if Christ has not been raised, then our preaching is vain [useless, amounting to nothing], and your faith is also vain [imaginary, unfounded, devoid of value and benefit—not based on truth].

(1 Corinthians 15:12-14)

At one funeral I attended in Africa, I saw a woman whose performance at the art of grieving could have earned her an Oscar, had this been a scene in a movie! Unfortunately, in some cases, reality is stranger than fiction. At the church funeral service, she was wailing uncontrollably, but the drama greatly intensified once we got to the burial site. I will never forget it as long as I live. As an impressionable teenager, I had never seen this before. I was completely captivated. Several times, this woman tried to throw herself into the burial pit together with the deceased's coffin!

Every single time she was about to throw herself into the burial pit on top of the coffin of the deceased, about four able-bodied men surrounded the burial pit and stopped her. All the while she was doing this, she was rebuking the deceased person for leaving her behind. She demanded that the deceased person take her with him because her life here on earth would be miserable without him. After five attempts to throw herself into the burial pit, the men stopping her got tired of intervening. So, on the sixth attempt, they all refused to intervene. So, when she got to the edge of the burial pit and realized that no one was preventing her from jumping into the pit, she suddenly stopped. She looked down at the coffin, cried some more, and then walked away to join the rest of the mourning party. I must say I was pretty disappointed. I was looking forward to her jumping into the burial pit just to see if the gravediggers were going to bury her alive with the deceased. I guess when she realized there was no one stopping her from jumping into the burial pit; it suddenly dawned on her that she wanted to live far more than she wanted to die!

However, when the Holy Spirit began to give me the revelation on the battle of altars, especially when He unveiled to me how a funeral altar operates, it suddenly dawned on me that this dramatic woman's ordeal did not end when the gravediggers buried the body of the deceased. When she went home, she actually left the gravesite, taking with her all the demons that were residing in the body of the now-deceased loved one. Her dramatic and senseless mourning of the deceased had given Satan all the legal rights he needed to enter her body. Most importantly, the Lord showed me that by asking the deceased person to take her with them, she willingly gave Satan the legal right in the Courts of Heaven to assign a spirit of death to her life. This is because out of her own mouth, she had invited the spirit of the dead, or the spirit of death, to come upon her. Next time you're at the funeral of the righteous dead, and most especially if the deceased was not a born-again Christian, you need to be very careful how you behave yourself around the funeral altar. I am convinced that demons love to hang around funerals, because this is when men and women are emotionally vulnerable to demonic penetration.

The Resurrection of the Dead

For the Lord Himself will come down from heaven with a shout of command, with the voice of the [a]archangel and with the [blast of the] trumpet of God, and the dead in Christ will rise first. [17]Then we who are alive and remain [on the earth] will simultaneously be caught up (raptured) together with them [the resurrected ones] in the clouds to meet the Lord in the air, and so we will always be with the Lord! [18]Therefore comfort and encourage one another with these words [concerning our reunion with believers who have died].

(1 Thessalonians 4:17-18)

In light of what we have just exposed about funeral altars, there is no biblical doctrine more important than the resurrection of the dead. Since the question of the soul's mortality is on the minds of all men, it is refreshing for the born-again Christian to realize that the Bible presents the resurrection of the righteous dead in a very positive light. The Apostle Paul goes out of his way to explain this glorious future event. He tells us that the Lord Himself will come down from heaven with a shout of command, with the voice of the Archangel and a blast of the trumpet of God, and the dead in Christ will rise first! This is exciting by any stretch of the imagination. Knowing and realizing that all those who have died in Christ will one day descend in the clouds with the Lord Jesus leading the way is exciting! Wow! In 1 Corinthians 15, Paul makes it abundantly clear if there is no resurrection of the dead, then our faith is useless. That is a strong statement that should inspire all believers in Christ.

ɷɷɷ

Demons love to hang around funerals, because this is when men and women are emotionally vulnerable to demonic penetration.

ɷɷɷ

The Glory of a Godly Death!

Precious [and of great consequence] in the sight of the Lord, is the death of His godly ones [so He watches over them].

(Psalm 116:15)

King David, in the above passage of Scripture, adds a poetic and beautiful rendition of what happens at the death of the righteous. King David makes it clear that God is the most excited when the righteous redeemed die. It's not because God is celebrating death. It is because God is not a God of the dead but the living. In essence, God is simply celebrating the safe arrival of one of His dear children into their eternal home. These are people who would have otherwise gone to hell into the pit of eternal damnation had they not made the righteous choice to follow God during their earthly pilgrimage. I believe a glory is released when the righteous ones die and go to be with their heavenly Father. So, if you have lost a loved one who died in the Lord, I want you to know that not only are you going to see them again, but their death was precious in the sight of the Lord. Praise God! This Scripture changed how I mourn during the funerals of deceased brothers and sisters in the Lord whom I loved and respected.

Tithing into a Funeral Altar!

I have not eaten from the tithe while mourning, nor have I removed any of it when I was [ceremonially] unclean [making the tithe ceremonially unclean], nor offered any of it to the dead. I have listened to the voice of the Lord my God; I have done everything in accordance with all that You have commanded me.

(Deuteronomy 26:14)

I could not believe that the above passage of Scripture was actually in the Bible. How can anyone tithe while mourning? This was a fascinating concept for me when I discovered it. Look at this sentence from the above biblical passage: *"I have not eaten from the tithe while mourning, nor have I removed any of it when I was [ceremonially] unclean [making the tithe ceremonially unclean], nor offered any of it to the dead."* What is the Holy Spirit talking about here? What does this verse mean when it admonishes the people of Israel not to eat the tithe while mourning, nor give it to the dead as an offering?

A flashlight of revelation went through my spirit when the Holy Spirit illuminated the mystery behind this verse. In the economy of God, the tithe represents the "first fruit" or the order of first things. The tithe is usually the first thing that comes out of the money that the Lord gives us. The Bible is very clear that the tithe is holy and that it belongs to the Lord! So, essentially this is what God is saying in this verse, "Don't finance a funeral of anyone using the Lord's tithe!" How many times have well-meaning Christians taken the Lord's tithe and used it to finance a funeral? According to the Holy Spirit and the biblical passage above, they are "eating the tithe" while mourning. Said simply, they are tithing into the dead! The Holy Spirit showed me that when God's children do this, they give legal rights to the spirit of death to come upon their finances. Maybe some of you reading this book just uncovered the mystery behind some of your financial struggles. I believe that if you repent and ask the blood of Jesus to forgive and cleanse you, God will remove the legal rights you gave to Satan to kill and steal your finances when you tithed into the dead. Wow, this is serious stuff!

Wakanda: Reviving Ancestral Worship!

When the people [instead of trusting God] say to you, "Consult the mediums [who try to talk to the dead] and the soothsayers who chirp and whisper and mutter," should not a people consult their God? Should they consult the dead-on behalf of the living?

(Isaiah 8:19)

Perhaps no movie has ever come out of Hollywood, especially out of the Marvel series, that has had more of a life-changing influence on Black people than the movie Black Panther. The main actor behind this blockbuster movie, Chadwick Boseman, known as King T'Challa in the movie, recently died from a four-year battle with cancer. A dear friend of mine who is a prophet in California was Chadwick's pastor. Many people, especially in Hollywood, did not know that Chadwick Boseman was a believer in Christ Jesus. One day I was driving with Prophet Gershom in California when Chadwick called him seeking prayer support for his battle with cancer. My heart went out to him, and we passionately prayed for him in the car. We both wanted him to be healed by the power of God.

Unfortunately, the healing we sought never took place. Chadwick died at the tender age of 43 years. When I got the news, I was heartbroken. Chadwick meant so much to so many people, especially to the Black community in America. They were still basking in the glory and aftermath of the fantastic success of the Black Panther movie. However, I was not ready for what God told me in my distress when I asked Him why He did not heal Chadwick Boseman from cancer that took his life. Here is what God told me: "I judged him in the flesh so that his spirit can be saved. Unknowingly, Satan used him and many of the actors in that movie to unleash the "spirit of ancestral worship" among Black Americans. So, in My mercy, I took him, as many Black people were beginning to idolize him, because of their obsession with the Black Panther movie." I was stunned, speechless!

I remember that some Black American pastors were so taken by the movie that they told their congregation to come to church dressed like Wakandans.

158

Most importantly, I heard many black leaders and activists make an appeal to their dead ancestors to watch over them. As a matter of fact, Gayle King hosted a documentary about the life and death of Chadwick Boseman. One of the celebrities on the video made this statement, "Chadwick has now become one of our ancestors watching over us!" Frankly speaking, I have never seen the spirit of ancestral worship become so popular among Black Americans until the movie Black Panther. In the movie, Chadwick Boseman dies temporarily and after being mortally wounded by the character played by Michael B. Jordan. Chadwick's character, King T'Challa, was eventually resurrected from the dead by consulting with his ancestors' spirits in the land of the dead.

Anubis, the Egyptian god of Death!

"Then the spirit of the Egyptians will become exhausted within them and emptied out; and I will confuse their strategy, so that they will consult the idols and the spirits of the dead, and mediums and soothsayers.

(Isaiah 19:3)

According to Wikipedia, Anubis in Ancient Egyptian is the Greek name of the god of death, mummification, embalming, the afterlife, cemeteries, tombs, and the Underworld. In ancient Egyptian religion, Anubis is usually depicted as a canine or a man with a canine head. This passage from the book of Isaiah is letting us know the grave danger that will befall us or anyone who gets caught up in any kind of ancestral worship. Once again, here is a why: how we behave around a funeral altar is very important. Most importantly, we need to make sure that we also behave accurately and righteously when we visit the tombstones of deceased loved ones at the cemetery during memorial services.

Anubis was a highly exalted deity in ancient Egyptian culture. Under the evil influence of this demonic deity, the Egyptians became experts at the art of embalming, mummification, and ceremonies that had to do with the underworld and the afterlife. That would explain why God, in His mercy, did not allow the children of Israel fresh from the idolatry of Egypt, bury the body of Moses when he died. In His eternal foreknowledge, God knew that the devil was planning on causing the children of Israel to stumble, spiritually speaking. Satan was going to trap them into a curse by tempting them to embalm Moses' dead body and by turning it into one of Israel's deities or idols. It is abundantly clear from what happened when Moses found them worshipping the golden calf that some of the children of Israel who came out of Egypt were still deep into idol worship.

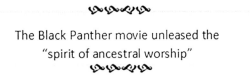

The Black Panther movie unleased the
"spirit of ancestral worship"

Jesus Delivered Us from the Power of Death!

Therefore, since [these His] children share in flesh and blood [the physical nature of mankind], He Himself in a similar manner also shared in the same [physical nature, but without sin], so that through [experiencing] death He might make powerless (ineffective, impotent) him who had the power of death—that is, the devil— [15] and [that He] might free all those who through [the haunting] fear of death were held in slavery throughout their lives.

(Hebrews 2:14-15)

Thankfully, for all of us, the above passage of Scripture shows us that Jesus, the Messiah, delivered us from the power of death. Praise God! The writer of the Book of Hebrews tells us that Jesus took the form of a man, that is to say, "flesh and blood," to condemn sin in the flesh and break the power of death. In so doing, Jesus also broke the power of the devil because death was his primary power. Since Adam's fall, Satan has successfully used the rod of the power of death to oppress and control generations of men, women, and children.

In dying, Jesus destroyed him who had the power of death (the devil) that he might free all of us who, through the fear of death, were held in slavery, bondage, and captivity. The Bible tells us that fear has torment. When you live in fear, you're actually being tormented by Satan. However, the strongman spirit behind the spirit of fear is death. That is why people who are afraid of dying often die early. Instead of being spared, they attract the spirit of death by their constant fear of it. I have good news for you. Jesus has set us free from living under the spirits of death and fear.

The Cloud of Witnesses: God is not the God of the Dead!

Therefore we also, since we are surrounded by so great a cloud of witnesses, let us lay aside every weight, and the sin which so easily ensnares us, and let us run with endurance the race that is set before us, 2 looking unto Jesus, the author and finisher of our faith, who for the joy that was set before Him endured the cross, despising the shame, and has sat down at the right hand of the throne of God.

(Hebrews 12:1-2, NKJV)

One of the most vital voices or witnesses in the Courts of Heaven is what the Bible refers to as the cloud of witnesses. This is where it gets weird and rather tricky because talking about the cloud of witnesses seems to borderline on the worship of the dead, which God sternly condemns in the entire old covenant. However, the difference is that ancestral worship is when people try to contact or consult with the spirits of the unrighteous dead. In contrast, the cloud of witnesses is a spiritual dimension in the heavenly realms where God can sovereignly take us. This is where we can receive the witness of some of the saints who slept in Christ here on earth but are very much alive in heaven in the presence of God. Please remember, the Lord Jesus already told us that God is not a God of the dead but the living.

But you have come to Mount Zion and to the city of the living God, the heavenly Jerusalem, and to myriads of angels [in festive gathering], ²³and to the general assembly and assembly of the firstborn who are registered [as citizens] in heaven, and to God, who is Judge of all, and to the spirits of the righteous (the redeemed in heaven) who have been made perfect [bringing them to their final glory],

(Hebrews 12:24)

Most importantly, when encountering or experiencing the cloud of witnesses, we must understand that the Bible says through the finished work of Christ and our union with Him, we have already come to Mount Zion, the city of the living God. It is the heavenly Jerusalem, the place where we find millions of angels in festive gatherings. Mount Zion is also where we find the assembly of the righteous redeemed spirits whose names are written in the Lamb's Book of Life. People involved in ancestral worship are not in the same spiritual dimension as the spirits of the unrighteous dead.

Consequently, to contact their dead ancestors, they would have had to consult with, or conjure up, demons from the underworld. Even then, the spiritual encounters they would have would most likely be with the familiar spirits that resided in their dead loved ones.

But concerning the raising of the dead, have you not read in the book of Moses, in the passage about the burning bush, how God spoke to him, saying, 'I am the God of Abraham, and the God of Isaac, and the God of Jacob'? 27He is not the God of the dead, but of the living; you are greatly mistaken, and you are deceiving yourselves!"

(Mark 12:26-27)

In the above passage of Scripture, Jesus makes it very clear that the God we serve, the God of Abraham, Isaac, and Jacob, is not a God of the dead but the living! So, Abraham is not dead. He's alive in heaven. Isaac is not dead. He's very much alive in heaven and so forth. That is why born-again Christians who, by God's sovereign choice, have had supernatural encounters with saints who are already in heaven have told me there was no weird feeling when they encountered these glorified saints. In contrast to the hair crawling on the back of one's neck if one encounters a ghost (disembodied, illegal spirit).

God is not the God of the dead!

Moses and Elijah minister to Jesus from the Cloud of Witnesses

Now about eight days after these teachings, He took along Peter and John and James and went up on the mountain to pray. [29]As He was praying, the appearance of His face became different [actually transformed], and His clothing became white and flashing with the brilliance of lightning. [30]And behold, two men were talking with Him; and they were Moses and Elijah, [31]who appeared in glory, and were speaking of His departure [from earthly life], which He was about to bring to fulfillment at Jerusalem.

(Luke 9:28-31)

If the cloud of witnesses was not a reality and essential to helping ministers of the gospel finish their God-given mandates here on earth, the above story would not make sense at all. Jesus knew that His time to go to the cross and become the sacrificial Lamb had come. In preparation for the sufferings He was about to endure — his death, burial, and resurrection — Jesus went to Mount Carmel to pray. He took three of His most trusted disciples: Peter, James, and John. Somewhere along His intense time of prayer, Jesus stepped into the dimension of the cloud of witnesses. He was immediately transformed before their eyes. The appearance of His face became different. His clothing became white, flashing with the brilliance of lightning as He manifested Himself in His glory, where there is no time dimension, the distance between heaven and earth collapsed.

In that sacred moment of the God encounter, Moses and Elijah appeared to Him in the glory. They began to speak to him about His departure from earthly life and the fulfillment of the prophecies spoken in Scripture concerning the Messiah. What is of note from the above passage of Scripture is that the cloud of witnesses of Moses and Elijah did not violate God's written word. They actually quoted what is written in the Holy Scriptures. Again, this is the critical difference between encountering the cloud of witnesses under the power of Christ and those consulting the spirits of their dead ancestors. The latter group does so outside of the realm of Scripture.

The Cloud of Witnesses and a Church Fully Awake!

Now Peter and those who were with him had been overcome with sleep; but when they were fully awake, they saw His glory and splendor and majesty, and the two men who were standing with Him. [33]And as these [men, Moses and Elijah] were leaving Him, Peter said to Jesus, "Master, it is delightful and good for us to be here; we should make three [sacred] tents; one for You, one for Moses, and one for Elijah"— not realizing what he was saying.

(Luke 9:32-33)

As the Church gets closer to the imminent return of the Lord Jesus Christ, God is going to send a sweeping revival by the Holy Spirit, and the Body of Christ will become spiritually awake. What happened to Peter is going to happen to the end-time Church. The Body of Christ-the Messiah on earth is going to become fully awake.

When Peter, James, and John were "fully awake," they saw His glory! They also saw Moses and Elijah ministering to Jesus from the cloud of witnesses. Peter was so overwhelmed by what he was seeing and experiencing. He suggested that they stay on the mountain and build three tents: one for Jesus, one for Moses, and the other for Elijah. Please note: Peter never said, the ghosts of Moses and Elijah, because they were very much alive. In an earlier chapter, I have already shared how God used my mother, Esther, from the cloud of witnesses to dismantle an evil altar from my father's side of the bloodline.

ভাৰভাৰ

God is going to send a sweeping revival by the Holy
Spirit, and the Body of Christ will become
spiritually awake.

ভাৰভাৰ

PRAYER OF ACTIVATION!

"Heavenly Father, I ask for the Court of Heaven to be seated and for the books of my destiny to be opened as I come before the Judge of all the earth to plead my case against any evil altar in my life or bloodline that is speaking against me. I decree and declare that the Holy Spirit is my official guide and counselor in this courtroom. Heavenly Father, I surrender all rights to self-representation; instead, I ask my defense attorney and mediator of the new covenant, the Lord Jesus Christ, to represent me in your Royal Courtroom against all idols and evil altars that are controlling my life and bloodline, in any way. I also ask the Lord Jesus to heal me by His blood from all soul wounds caused by idols and evil altars in my bloodline. I am seeking a verdict of release from the power of these evil altars in Jesus' Name.

I now enter a plea of 'guilty' into the court's records concerning any legitimate accusations that Satan has filed in Court against me or my bloodline. For Jesus said, in Matthew 5:25, *"Come to terms quickly [at the earliest opportunity] with your opponent at law while you are with him on the way [to court], so that your opponent does not hand you over to the judge, and the judge to the guard, and you are thrown into prison."* Lord, since I am under oath, I cannot lie about my sinful activities and the iniquities of my bloodline that are connected to idolatry and the erecting evil altars. I repent for all sins and transgressions that I and my ancestors ever committed against you and the laws of nature. I repent for any time I took the Lord's tithe and gave it to the dead. Cleanse me from all sin by the blood of Jesus, according to 1 John 1:9. I now formally submit my guilty plea and repentance to the court, in Jesus' Name."

Heavenly Father,

- I decree and declare that the power of any funeral altar is completely destroyed in Jesus' Name!
- I decree and declare that the Lord Jesus has set me free from the law of sin and death, so death has no power of me, in Jesus' Name!
- I decree and declare that every family member who is tied to a funeral altar is now free in Jesus' Name!
- I decree and declare that the spirit of resurrection is upon my life, in Jesus' Name!
- I decree and declare that you are setting me free from idols that cause people to be physically or spiritually crippled in Jesus' Name!
- I decree and declare that I am completely healed from all soul wounds connected to any funeral altar in my bloodline, in Jesus' Name!
- I decree and declare that Anubis, the Egyptian god of death, has no power over me, so I will not die before my appointed time, in Jesus' Name!

LIFE APPLICATION
Memory Verse

For we know that if the earthly tent [our physical body] which is our house is torn down [through death], we have a building from God, a house not made with hands, eternal in the heavens. 2For indeed in this house we groan, longing to be clothed with our [immortal, eternal] celestial dwelling, 3so that by putting it on we will not be found naked. 4For while we are in this tent, we groan, being burdened [often weighed down, oppressed], not that we want to be unclothed [separated by death from the body], but to be clothed, so that what is mortal [the body] will be swallowed up by life [after the resurrection].

(2 Corinthians 5:1-4)

Reflections

1. What is a funeral altar?

    _____
    _____
    _____
    _____

2. Why is it important for people of faith to behave properly around a funeral altar?

    _____
    _____
    _____
    _____

An altar is a place of worship.

10

Music Idols & Altars

Nebuchadnezzar the king made a gold [-plated] image, whose height [including the pedestal] was sixty cubits (ninety feet) and its width six cubits (nine feet). He set it up on the plain of Dura in the province of Babylon. ²Then Nebuchadnezzar the king sent word to assemble the [b]satraps, the prefects and the governors, the counselors, the treasurers, the judges, the magistrates and lawyers and all the chief officials of the provinces to come to the dedication of the image that King Nebuchadnezzar had set up.

(Daniel 3:1-2)

Without a doubt, one of the most influential altars (platforms) on earth is the altar of music. Music, more than any other influence in our culture, affects millions and millions of people. The truth of the matter is that we were designed by God to be animated by music. because we were created to worship God. It is clear from the teaching of Scripture that Lucifer was the leading worshipper in heaven before becoming Satan. The Book of Ezekiel tells us that on the day Lucifer was created, God built pipes of music into his body. So, without a doubt, there is no angelic being that God ever created who is animated by the sound of music and its lingering effect on the soul more than Lucifer, commonly known as Satan.

169

In the above passage of Scripture, I wanted you to note that King Nebuchadnezzar connected the worship of the golden idol to the sound of music. This chapter will show you the spiritual and mysterious connection between music, idols, and evil altars.

The Connection between Idolatry and Music

Then the satraps, the prefects, the governors, the counselors, the treasurers, the judges, the magistrates and lawyers, and all the chief officials of the provinces gathered together for the dedication of the image that King Nebuchadnezzar had set up; and they stood before it. ⁴Then the herald loudly proclaimed, "You are commanded, O peoples, nations, and speakers of every language, ⁵that at the moment you hear the sound of the horn, pipe, lyre, trigon (four-stringed harp), dulcimer, bagpipe, and all kinds of music, you are to fall down and worship the golden image that King Nebuchadnezzar has set up.

(Daniel 3:3-5)

There is a deep and mystical connection between music and the spirit of worship. It's almost impossible to separate music from worship. While the secular culture we live in sees music as a form of entertainment, the truth of the matter is one cannot validate that approach to music within the Canon of Scripture. In the Bible, music is rarely ever connected to entertainment but to worship. The reason is obvious: God created music and gave it tremendous power over man's soul for the sole purpose of enabling man to worship the God who created him. However, the fall of the angel of worship, Lucifer, followed by the fall of Adam and Eve in the Garden, compromised and perverted God's purpose for creating music.

I will never forget the images of men and women fawning and fainting at the sight of the King of Pop music, Michael Jackson. These men and women were acting as if they had lost their minds and all moral restraint. They looked at Michael Jackson with worshipful eyes, as if he was the second coming of Jesus Christ. Many of them cried as they screamed at the top of their voice, "Michael,

Michael!" It was clear to me that he was more than a music entertainer to many of Michael Jackson's fans; he had become their idol.

Interestingly, the most popular music competition in the world was branded, American Idol. This music contest, headed by the legendary Simon Cowell, took the world by storm and captured young people's imagination. Young men and women hoping to become the next music idol entered the cutthroat competition to reach American Idol's finals.

Whether Simon Cowell and the other American Idol creators knew it or not, the cat was out of the bag. What they revealed is that there is a deep spiritual connection between music and idolatry in our modern culture. Needless to say, wherever there is an "idol," you don't have to look very far to find the altar (platform) the idol operates from to command worship from its human attendants. During American Idol, for instance, the judges sat on a table on the same level as the rest of the crowd. However, the contestants were placed on a "high place." In biblical times, the altars of the Lord, or altars to demonic deities, were almost always placed on high places. These high places were high geographical places such as mountains or hills. In the Bible, rarely was an altar placed in a valley, hence the constant reference to high places in Scripture.

Consequently, over the natural course of time, altars became known as high places. In the chapter on "Defining an Altar," I mentioned that an altar is a platform where God or demons can land to exact worship from the gathered assembly of human attendants.

Back to American Idol: the contestants were placed on an altar (platform). They built into the platform all the glitz and glamour we associate with celebrities. From this altar or platform, the starry-eyed contestants were expected to perform for the judges and the crowd to see who would become the next American music idol.

It is clear from the passage we read from the Book of Daniel that King Nebuchadnezzar understood the mysterious and spiritual connection between music and the worship of idols. This is why in his royal proclamation, he made it clear that the citizens of his kingdom could not commence with the worship of the golden idol he had set-up until they heard the sound of music.

వావావావావ

God created music and gave it tremendous power over the soul of man for the sole purpose of enabling man to worship the God who created him.

వావావావావ

Worshipping Demons at the Altar of Music

Whoever does not fall down and worship shall immediately be thrown into the midst of a furnace of blazing fire." [7]*So when the people heard the sound of the horn, pipe, lyre, trigon, dulcimer, bagpipe and all kinds of music, all the peoples, nations, and speakers of every language fell down and worshiped the golden image that Nebuchadnezzar the king had set up.*

(Daniel 3:6-7)

Without a shadow of a doubt, the Bible does not hide the fact that idols are simply demon-gods or fallen angels hiding behind a "physical image or soulish desire" to cause the souls of men to bow down in worship to Satan. Satan has always wanted to be worshipped as God. In other words, worshipping idols is the equivalent of worshipping demons. There is simply no way to sugarcoat this. King Nebuchadnezzar knew this. Consequently, in his royal proclamation, he told his nobles, officers, satraps, and all the Babylon people that when they heard the stringed instruments, the harp, and all kinds of music instruments, they should bow down in worship to the golden image bearing his face. In his desire to be like God, Satan demands that every form of music and instrument that is used in heaven to worship God to be directed to worship him here on earth.

It's no wonder Satan goes out of his way to promote as "idols" many of our legendary music icons. The music industry is replete with the excessive usage of drugs, alcohol, and participation in illicit sexual activities because all of these practices were an integral part of worshiping demons in biblical times. Children of God everywhere must be careful and prayerful about what music they listen to (and what they allow their children to listen to), most especially if the artist behind the music is secular.

The altar of music is too powerful for Satan to allow an artist to remain uncompromised on the platform if he or she is not entirely sold-out to Jesus Christ. Satan will quickly hijack their God-given gift of music, transform them into an idol, and then use them to receive worship for himself. If you listen to them, most of the music lyrics by secular artists are very idolatrous in nature. They usually contain phrases like, "I cannot live without you" or "I am nothing without you." These phrases only make sense if the object of worship is God. However, in most cases, these music divas and popstars are singing about another human being, which is, in essence, the worship of self. The truth of the matter is that the worship of self is simply a disguised form of Luciferian worship.

Children of God everywhere must be careful and prayerful about what music they are listening to!

All Evil Altars Demand Worship

At that time certain Chaldeans came forward and brought [malicious] accusations against the Jews. ⁹They said to King Nebuchadnezzar, "O king, live forever! ¹⁰You, O king, have made a decree that everyone who hears the sound of the horn, pipe, lyre, trigon, harp, dulcimer, bagpipe, and all kinds of music is to fall down and worship the golden image. ¹¹Whoever does not fall down and worship shall be thrown into the midst of a furnace of blazing fire. ¹²There are certain Jews whom you have appointed over the administration of the province of Babylon, namely Shadrach, Meshach, and Abednego. These men, O king, pay no attention to you; they do not serve your gods or worship the golden image which you have set up." ¹³Then Nebuchadnezzar in a furious rage gave a command to bring Shadrach, Meshach, and Abednego; and these men were brought before the king. [14]Nebuchadnezzar said to them, "Is it true, Shadrach, Meshach, and Abednego, that you do not serve my gods or worship the golden image which I have set up?

(Daniel 3:8-14)

Whether King Nebuchadnezzar knew it or not, both God and Satan were using him to send a message that the currency of life on earth is worship. After King Nebuchadnezzar set-up the altar of the golden image, he demanded his citizens bow down to this evil altar and the idol it contained. The three Hebrew boys, Shadrach, Meshach, and Abednego, were high ranking officers in King Nebuchadnezzar's government. They knew that if they bowed down in worship at the altar of the golden image, they would, be renouncing their spiritual allegiance to the God of Abraham, Isaac, and Jacob. That, they knew they could not do. So, when the Babylonian musicians began to play every instrument of music in honor of the golden image, all the Babylonians bowed down in worship. The only ones standing were the three Hebrew boys. King Nebuchadnezzar's officers, who saw their defiance of the king's edict, were outraged. They ran to the king's palace to report the defiance of the king's edict by these Jewish captives.

Shadrach, Meshach, and Abednego were quickly brought into the presence of a furious king. King Nebuchadnezzar questioned the validity of the accusations that had been brought against them by his other officials. To his dismay, the Hebrew boys confirmed the fact that the accusations were true. So, the king gave them another opportunity to worship at the altar of the golden image at the next sound of music. In holy defiance, Shadrach, Meshach, and Abednego told the king that they were willing to die for their faith and conviction in the God of Abraham, Isaac, and Jacob. At no time were they going to bow down at the altar of the golden image.

Outraged, King Nebuchadnezzar commanded that they be thrown into the burning furnace to be burned to death. Then the unthinkable happened. Once they were thrown into the burning furnace that had been heated seven times hotter, King Nebuchadnezzar saw a miracle he had never seen before!

Shadrach, Meshach, and Abednego were walking and worshipping God in the midst of the fire unscathed and unscorched. Most important, it was the sight of the fourth man in the fire who looked like the "Son of God" that captivated King Nebuchadnezzar. He called for the three Hebrew boys to be taken out of the fire. When they came out of the burning furnace, to the utter amazement of King Nebuchadnezzar and all the Babylonians, they were unscathed by the fire. The smoke and fire had not even touched their clothes! In a complete reversal of fortune, King Nebuchadnezzar ended up bowing in worshipful adoration to the God of Abraham, Isaac, and Jacob. Shadrach, Meshach, and Abednego had thwarted the desire of King Nebuchadnezzar's evil altar for worship.

Unmasking the gods behind the Music

Now if you are ready, when you hear the sound of the horn, pipe, lyre, trigon, harp, dulcimer, and all kinds of music, to fall down and worship the image which I have made, very good. But if you do not worship, you shall be thrown at once into the midst of a furnace of blazing fire; and what god is there who can rescue you out of my hands?" [16]Shadrach, Meshach, and Abednego answered the king, "O Nebuchadnezzar, we do not need to answer you on this point. [17]If it be so, our God whom we serve is able to rescue us from the furnace of blazing fire, and He will rescue us from your hand, O king. [18]But even if He does not, let it be known to you, O king, that we are not going to serve your gods or worship the golden image that you have set up!"

(Daniel 3:15-18)

I want you to note that even though King Nebuchadnezzar kept referencing bowing to the golden image that he had created, he knew intuitively that the entire exercise was about the worship of the gods of the Babylonians. Most importantly, the three Hebrew boys were not deceived about what was at stake. They had unmasked what was actually behind the entire exercise. It was the worship of the demon-gods of the Babylonians. Interestingly enough, the Babylonians included King Nebuchadnezzar among the gods of the land.

Notice how King Nebuchadnezzar emphasizes the different kinds of music and instruments in the above passage of Scripture.

It appears that there is a demon-god behind every genre of music if the attendants to the altar are not worshipping the true and living God. Heavy metal and rock and roll, for instance, seem to be connected to "Anubis," the ancient Egyptian god of death. Heavy metal and rock and roll music have been connected to death through drug overdose, suicide, and even murder. May God give us the spirit of discernment to discern many of the demon-gods that are lurking behind the different streams of music that are bombarding our senses at most public places. Some heavy metal lyrics of some rock and roll bands call for the worship of Lucifer.

Jezebel and the Altar of Music

But an opportune time [finally] came [for Herodias]. Herod on his birthday gave a banquet for his officials (nobles, courtiers) and military commanders and the leading men of Galilee. ²²Now [Salome] the daughter of Herodias came in and danced [for the men]. She pleased and beguiled Herod and his dinner guests; and the king said to the girl, "Ask me for whatever you want and I will give it to you." ²³And he swore to her, "Whatever you ask me, I will give it to you; up to half of my kingdom." ²⁴She went out and said to her mother, "What shall I ask for?" And Herodias replied, "The head of John the Baptist!"

(Mark 6:21-24)

The above passage of Scripture is both tragic and revealing. Most important, it shows the mysterious connection between music, dance, and the spirit of Jezebel. We all know from Scripture that Jezebel is a prophetic representation of a controlling, seductive spirit that hates the prophetic voice of God. John the Baptist, whom Jesus said was the Elijah to come, and the greatest prophet to come out of the womb of a woman, was languishing in a Jewish prison. King Herod had placed him in jail after John rebuked him for marrying his brother's wife, Herodias. Herodias, who had a Jezebel spirit, never forgave him for challenging the sanctity of her marriage to the king.

According to the above passage of Scripture, there came a time during King Herod's birthday that an opportunity presented itself for Herodias to exact her revenge. An intoxicated King Herod wanted to provide his esteemed guests with some entertainment. So, he summoned Salome, Herodias' daughter, to dance before them. She was a very seductive dancer who could arouse the sexual passions of men and women as she danced. To rightly divide the word of truth, you have to read between the lines. There is no way Salome was doing a dry dance before the king. Even though the Bible does not say it, it implies that she was dancing to the sound of music as she entertained Herod and his guests with her highly seductive dances. Have you noticed that most people find it difficult to dance without the sound of music? It is unnatural and does not last very long.

The sound of music creates a nostalgic feeling in the soul of man. When combined with the sensual dance moves of a professional seductress, this nostalgic feeling is very powerful. Men and women find themselves powerless to resist the seductive influence of the seducing spirit that is animating the entire experience. That is what happened when Salome began to dance to the sound of music. When she was done, Herod and his guests were drooling with lust. Deeply moved, King Herod blurted out these words and swore to her, "Whatever you ask me, I will give it to you; up to half of my kingdom."

May God give us the spirit of discernment to discern many of the demon-gods that are lurking behind the different streams of music that are bombarding our senses

Mesmerized by the power yielded by the evil spirit working through her to seduce these powerful men, Salome took the king's request to her mother. She asked her mother, Herodias, what she should ask from the king. You would have thought a young lady at her age would have asked for half of the kingdom or money to take her on a shopping spree. Instead, her mother told her to ask for the head of John the Baptist on a silver platter. This passage of Scripture proves beyond any reasonable doubt that one of the tools in Jezebel's weaponry involves using the double-barreled gun of music and dance to kill the prophetic flow of God in a generation.

Music Lyrics that Kill!

And she rushed back to the king and asked, saying, "I want you to give me right now the head of John the Baptist on a platter!" [26]The king was deeply grieved, but because of his oaths and his dinner guests [who might have regarded him as weak], he was unwilling to [break his word and] refuse her. [27]So the king immediately sent for an executioner and commanded him to bring back John's head. And he went and had John beheaded in the prison, [28]and brought back his head on a platter, and gave it to the girl; and the girl gave it to her mother. [29]When his disciples heard about this, they came and took away John's body and laid it in a tomb.

(Mark 6:21-29)

The story of King Herod, Herodias, Salome, and John the Baptist proves that there exist in this world music that can be weaponized to kill or drive people into a demonic frenzy. Had King Herod known that Herodias and Salome had weaponized her music and dance to cause him to do the unthinkable — kill John the Baptist — he would never have called her to perform. Most important, he would never have vowed to give her whatever she desired, up to half his kingdom. Unfortunately, by the time he discovered what the spirit of Jezebel had done in plotting the assassination of John the Baptist by his very command, it was too late to reverse the conspiracy!

While Herodias and Salome are long-dead, the demons that inspired them to use music and dance to kill the prophet of God are still alive and well in today's society! They live in different human hosts, who control much of what goes on in the music industry. All you have to do is spend time on a Google search, and you'll be shocked at the number of teenagers who have committed murder or suicide after listening to the murderous lyrics of a music icon who had weaponized their music. The following story is presented here to unmask this dark side of music.

"The debate over the social impact of gangsta rap music moves to a Milwaukee courtroom Wednesday when two Wisconsin minors will be charged with murder in the country's second case of rap allegedly inspiring the killing of a police officer. The case involves two teens who told authorities they plotted a Sept. 7 sniper attack on a police van "because of a Tupac Shakur record that talks about killing the police." The assault resulted in the shooting death of 31-year-old Milwaukee Police Officer William A. Robertson. The 17-year-old defendants, Curtis Lee Walker and Denziss Jackson, will be tried as adults in a case that is expected to reach trial before the end of the year. They have been held without bail at the Milwaukee County Children's Court Center since their arrest and were unavailable for comment."[1] Los Angeles Times, 1994

Music Divas and their Alter Egos

But the [Holy] Spirit explicitly and unmistakably declares that in later times some will turn away from the faith, paying attention instead to deceitful and seductive spirits and doctrines of demons.

(1 Timothy 4:1)

It is amazing how deep and far-reaching this message on altars really goes. In an earlier chapter, I mentioned that no one could have real spiritual power, God's or the devil's, without standing on an altar. In essence, the spirit animating a speaker, politician, or musician can be quickly revealed by observing how they behave when they are on stage (altar). Recently there has been a growing trend of music icons publicly revealing what is commonly known as their alter-ego. The phrase "alter-ego" is very interesting and revealing. First and foremost, it means that these music divas either consciously or unconsciously know that their performance on stage is connected to an altar and the idol behind it.

Second, the phrase "alter-ego" is meant to convey two messages:

- The word "alter" in "alter-ego" is a musician's way of describing the "alteration" that transpires in their soul, voice, mannerisms, and dance moves while they are on stage.
- The word "ego" in "alter-ego" is a musician's way of describing the spirit entity that possesses their body and takes command of their voice and dance moves while they are on stage.

In essence, the artists know that the performance and celebrity status do not come from their God-given talent but the manipulation of the audience by their alter-ego.

Nikki Minaj is a very famous American music diva, originally from the beautiful islands of Trinidad and Tobago. She is the winner of several music awards, and some of her songs have reached the highly coveted platinum record status. Nikki Minaj's alter-ego is called "Roman." Below is an actual conversation between Nikki Minaj and a radio DJ who interviewed her as she was promoting her new album. It's chilling, to say the least.

Nikki: *"Roman is a crazy boy who lives in me. And he says the things that I don't want to say. He was born just a few months ago. I think he was born out of rage. He was conceived in rage. So, he bashes everyone and threatens to beat people. And he is violent."*

Radio DJ: *"That must be nice to have like an ignorant loudmouth who you can just sort of blame."*

Nikki: *"He wants to be blamed. I don't want to blame him. I asked him to leave, but he can't. He's here for a reason. People have brought him out. People conjured him up. Now he won't leave."*

Radio DJ: *"What is the situation with Roman's revenge?"*

Nikki: *"Right? Roman's revenge. Roman is just about taking control, saying Roman is here to stay and anybody that ever doubted Roman is going down in a coffin!"*[2]

If Nikki were a member of my church, I would have scheduled a deliverance session for her. This is a woman who is being used and oppressed by a demon called "Roman." It was not just an interview to promote a new album. If you read between the "lines," she is crying out for help while acting "cool." The Bible took the mask off the faces of demons and showed us that they are mean-spirited beings, incapable of loving humans. "Roman" is not in love with Nikki Minaj. As a messenger of Satan, this demon is on an assignment to pervert her God-given talent of singing. Once "Roman" is finished with Nikki Minaj, he is telling her that he will put her in a coffin and drag her soul to hell.

Unfortunately, pop culture is so prone to idolatry, occultism, and self-worship, people are blind to the danger of consorting with demons. For some of you parents who are letting your children listen to music by Nikki Minaj, she is forewarning you that the spirit behind her songs is "Roman." So why would you be surprised when your children suddenly turn violent? Nikki Minaj lets you know that "Roman" is an angry little boy who lives inside her who wants to beat people up.

Without any contradiction, there is no female music icon (diva) who is more worshipped than Beyonce! Beyonce's latest album, Black is King, pictures her with a goat's horns attached to her head. Whether she knows or not, it's an evil occultic symbol. It is the satanic symbol for the god known as "Baphomet." Many occultists refer to "Baphomet" as Lucifer! According to Wikipedia, a popular online encyclopedia:

> "Baphomet is a deity that the Knights Templar were accused of worshipping, and that subsequently was incorporated into occult and mystical traditions. The name Baphomet appeared in trial transcripts for the Inquisition of the Knights Templar starting in 1307. It first came into popular English usage in the 19th century during debate and speculation on the reasons for the suppression of the Templars.[3]

> Since 1856, the name Baphomet has been associated with the "Sabbatic Goat" image drawn by Éliphas Lévi, which contains binary elements representing the "symbolization of the equilibrium of opposites"

(e.g., half-human and half-animal, male and female, good and evil, on and off, etc.).On the one hand, Lévi intended to symbolize his concept of balance that was essential to his magnetitic notion of the Astral Light; on the other hand, the Baphomet represents a tradition that should result in a perfect social order."[4]

Below is a direct quote from the website Christianity.com about this ancient goat-god.

"We've often heard of goats being associated with witchcraft and Satan himself. The Bible never seems to have many good things to say about this creature (Matthew 25:31-46), so it should come as no surprise that one of the statues of the Satanic Temple, known as Baphomet, has a goat's head."[5]

Why in God's good name would an African American music icon, who grew up in a Christian family, produce an album with a cover that depicts her wearing the horns of a goat? I believe, at some level, she's crying out for deliverance, and at worst, she is telling her world of fans the god she now worships.

Beyonce Knowles' alter-ego is called "Sasha." Listen to Beyonce introduce the world to her alter-ego:

"When I performed Crazy in Love at the BET awards, it was almost like my coming out, ladies and gentlemen. And I remember when they told me I was performing on BET. In my mind, I saw the set immediately. I said, "I want something big. I want something that says I'm here." And I drew it out. I drew out the ramp. I drew out the boxes for me and my girls. I drew out the lift, right?! Oh, it just so happened that was right in the center of my name for me to come down. I knew the dance. I knew about the pumps. I saw all of that in my head before it happened. And it's great when you visualize something, and it actually comes to life.

It was way better than…I expected. And Sasha was in full effect. Sasha is my alter-ego. And when people see me, sometimes I think that when they meet me and they speak with me, they're expecting Sasha. And, I'm really kind of shy and not really shy, but more reserved. And, I am nothing like Sasha. I guess I wouldn't be very entertaining on the stage. So, Sasha comes out and she's fearless. She can, she can do things that I cannot do when I'm in rehearsal. I mean, I can try, but then it just doesn't happen. I can sing notes and sing strong and do all these things that when I'm just by myself, I can't do. I remember right before I performed. I raised my hands up and it was kind of the first time I felt something else come into me. And I knew that was going to be my coming out night."[5]

I want you to let Beyonce's own words "sink" deeply into your spirit and come to terms with what she is telling the world. Let us first examine her last statement in the quote, "I raised my hands up, and it was kind of the first time I felt something else come into me. And I knew that was going to be my coming out night." Every Bible reader who understands what the Bible says about demonology and how demonic spirits operate should be horrified by this statement. Beyonce is telling us of a moment in time in her desperate attempt to become famous when she opened her soul to be possessed by a demon she now calls, "Shasha."

According to her own confession, she knew that things would be different from that point on when this "thing" entered her body. She knew that that night's performance on the stage (altar) would be her coming out party! But this begs the question, Whose coming-out party was this, Sasha's or Beyonce Knowles?

༄‿ལ༄‿ལ‿ལ༄‿ལ

Unfortunately, "pop culture" is so prone towards idolatry, occultism and self-worship, they are blind to the danger of fraternizing with demons.

༄‿ལ༄‿ལ‿ལ༄‿ལ

As one used by God in the ministry of deliverance, let tell you what happened when Sasha met Beyonce. Please remember in a previous chapter, when I talked about mobile altars, I told you that when God meets with a man, an altar is born. But I also told you that when a demonic spirit meets with a human being and an exchange occurs, an evil altar is also born. Beyonce wanted to be famous at all costs, and Sasha, as an agent of Satan, needed to influence the souls of men. So, an exchange happened. Sasha got the vehicle of Beyonce's body to influence millions of people, and Beyonce' got the global fame in the music industry she so desperately desired.

Let us now examine another equally disturbing portion of Beyonce's statement concerning the difference between her and Sasha. Here is Beyonce in her own words. "And when people see me, sometimes I think that when they meet me and they speak with me, they're expecting Sasha. I'm really kind of shy and not really shy, but more reserved. I am nothing like Sasha. I guess I wouldn't be very entertaining on the stage. So, Sasha comes out and she's fearless. She can, she can do things that I cannot do when I'm in rehearsal. I mean, I can try, but then it just doesn't happen. I can sing notes and sing strong and do all these things that when I'm just by myself, I can't do."

You don't have to be a rocket scientist to read between the lines and figure out what Beyonce is saying. She's telling us that there is a marked difference in "personality" between her and Sasha. She's telling us that Sasha is a different personality from Beyonce's. The only 'personalities' mentioned in Scripture capable of possessing a human's body are called "demons." Listen to Jesus tell us about this phenomenon in Matthew 12:43-45:

"Now when the unclean spirit has gone out of a man, it roams through waterless (dry, arid) places in search of rest, but it does not find it. Then it says, 'I will return to my house from which I came.' And when it arrives, it finds the place unoccupied, swept, and put in order. Then it goes and brings with it seven other spirits more wicked than itself, and they go in and make their home there. And the last condition of that man becomes worse than the first. So, will it also be with this wicked generation."

Furthermore, Beyonce is also telling us that this personality she calls "Sasha' has supernatural abilities to sing and dance beyond her natural capabilities and talent as Beyonce Knowles. In other words, whether she knows it or not, her body has become a vehicle for this demonic entity called "Sasha." That is why when I see African American pastors act like little children in a candy store around Beyonce, I know for certain they lack spiritual discernment and have things in their soul that are in common with "Sasha."

Even Boxers have their Alter Egos

People who follow boxing know the legendary boxing match that took place between Deontay Wilder and Tyson Fury. Deontay Wilder was the crowd favorite, and betting odds had him winning the fight. However, the usual bombastic Deontay Wilder was beaten like a spoiled child on the day of the fight to the utter amazement of a sold-out arena! It was like watching an amateur take punches from the hard-hitting Tyson Fury. However, the mystery behind the poor boxing performance of Deontay Wilder is easily explained when you examine what happened between the two boxers in their pre-fight interview. Below is the exchange between the two boxers,

Deontay Wilder: *"When that night or that fight comes, you're not going to be talking to Deontay Wilder. You're not going to be looking in the eyes of Deontay Wilder."*

Tyson Fury: *"Who am I going to be looking in the eyes of?"*

Deontay Wilder: *You won't be looking in the eyes of the bronze bomber. You're going to feel them as well, too. Just like the feeling that you feel now."*

Tyson Fury: *"Is it like an alter ego or something, or is it a spirit that comes into you or what is it?"*

Deontay Wilder: *"It could be an alter ego, and it can be a spirit, or it may be an ancestral spirit who knows. I'm part Nigerian as well too."*

Tyson Fury: *"I don't believe in all that stuff."*

Deontay Wilder: *"I do."*

Tyson Fury: *"Because Jesus Christ is my savior, and I don't believe in all these spirits and alter egos. And even mentioning this stuff on TV you are going to get it. Nobody can be against me. And if you are already turning to spirits and allowing stuff into your body, you can't win. You've already lost. You can't beat me. I would say to you today as a sincere man, who tells the truth and hides nothing, behind no curtains, I'm baiting you 1000000%. I've not got no doubts. Even if after all the time off, you cannot beat me. When you look at me, I'm not lying. I'm not just doing it for the cameras or whatever. I know deep in my heart; you can't beat me. I don't know, if anyone can. I'll retire an unbeaten heavyweight champion of the world, like Rocky Marciano. The second man to do it in history. You can't beat me and 10 more like you can't beat me. I have something that goes back in history, hundreds of years, right here, the lineaship at the heavyweight division. And I know for a fact, you can't take it from me. I just know it. It's not what you do great or what you do wrong? I know deep in my heart. I can beat you."*

You will notice from the interaction between the two boxers that they represented two opposing kingdoms, the Kingdom of Light versus the kingdom of darkness. Wilder, the boxing world's favorite, admitted on national TV that he won his many fights through the strength of his alter-ego. In another interview, he named referenced the name of his alter-ego, the Bronze Bomber, an ancestral spirit! Since the boxing ring is also built like an altar (stage), once he was inside the ring, his "alter-ego" would do the fighting, using his body as a mere vehicle of his ancestral spirit. Unfortunately for Deontay Wilder, Tyson Fury was just not another boxer in the heavyweight division. He was an attendant to a higher and superior righteous altar. He is a strong believer and disciple of Jesus. In the "Battle of Altars," the altar Tyson Fury was standing on won the day! The result was a stunning defeat of Deontay Wilder that left the boxing world dumbfounded. Gamblers who had a lot of money riding on the odds of Deontay Wilder winning the fight against a much older Tyson Fury lost thousands of dollars. This story shows that not even the world of professional sports is free from the battle of altars.

Music Altars & Sexual Orgies

And he took the gold from their hands, and fashioned it with an engraving tool and made it into a molten calf; and they said, "This is your god, O Israel, who brought you up from the land of Egypt." 5Now when Aaron saw the molten calf, he built an altar before it; and Aaron made a proclamation, and said, "Tomorrow shall be a feast to the Lord!" 6So they got up early the next day and offered burnt offerings, and brought peace offerings; then the people sat down to eat and drink, and got up to play [shamefully—without moral restraint]… 17Now when Joshua heard the noise of the people as they shouted, he said to Moses, "There is a sound of battle in the camp." 18But Moses said, "It is not the sound of the cry of victory, Nor is it the sound of the cry of defeat; But I hear the sound of singing."

(Exodus 34:4-18)

One of the tragic events that transpired under Aaron's priesthood was the making of the golden calf in the wilderness and building an altar to it. This event became a permanent blemish on the priesthood of Aaron. If you follow this story from its inception, Aaron was reluctant to create the golden calf while Moses was on the mountain seeking the face of God. However, the people continued to pressure him because they were idol worshippers and needed an idol to worship. The million-dollar question is, "Why did Aaron succumb to the peer pressure to create an idol and build an altar to a demon-god?" It's because Aaron had something "in-common" in his soul with the spirit of idolatry.

How did Aaron know to make idols in the first place? He learned the art of making idols while living in Egypt. Egyptians were devout idol worshippers. It is interesting to note that after Aaron built the golden calf and set it up on an altar, he became deceived and mistook the idol for the Lord God of Abraham, Isaac, and Jacob. That is quite interesting and revealing. It exposes the primary intent of idols. It is to replace God in your life until you don't see the difference between serving the Living God and worshipping the idol created by your own hands. Once the golden idol and the altar were in full operation, spirits of seduction fell upon the people.

As the festivities continued, they worshiped the golden idol through music, song, and dance. The men and women lost all morals and self-restraint and began to participate in sexual orgies publicly. The sexual orgies are not implicitly mentioned in the biblical passage but are directly implied in the phrase, "…people began to behave shamefully without moral restraint." This biblical passage establishes the spiritual connection between idols, music altar, and sexual orgies. It is imperative to note that it is a well-known fact that most occultic practices include sexual orgies.

The Power of an Anointed Music Altar

Now the Spirit of the Lord departed from Saul, and an evil spirit from the Lord tormented and terrified him. [15]Saul's servants said to him, "Behold, an evil spirit from God is tormenting you. [16]Let our lord now command your servants who are here before you to find a man who plays skillfully on the harp; and when the evil spirit from God is on you, he shall play the harp with his hand, and you will be well." [17]So Saul told his servants, "Find me a man who plays well and bring him to me." [18]One of the young men said, "Behold, I have seen a son of Jesse the Bethlehemite who is a skillful musician, a brave

and competent man, a warrior, discerning (prudent, eloquent) in speech, and a
handsome man; and the Lord is with him."

(1 Samuel 16:14-18)

I would be remiss if I ended a chapter on "Music Idols and Evil Altars" without dealing with their supernatural counterpart in the Kingdom of God, namely, righteous music altars. Once again, I want you to remember that when God meets with a man who fully surrenders his life to Him, a righteous mobile altar is born. The first time in the Bible we hear of David, his name is never mentioned, but it is implied when the Prophet Samuel told a disobedient King Saul that God had found for Himself "a man after His own heart." So, it is clear by rightly dividing the word of truth that David had a supernatural encounter with God long before Samuel showed up to anoint him as the next king of Israel.

In other words, David, the anointed psalmist, musician, and shepherd, was a righteous mobile altar long before King Saul came looking for the soothing power of music from a righteous altar.

It is important to notice the difference between music's effect from a righteous altar versus an evil altar. Music from a righteous altar refreshes the soul by driving out the presence of demonic spirits. Every time a tormenting spirit entered the body of King Saul, his servants would send for David to play soothing music from his harp. The Bible says as soon as David started playing the harp, the supernatural energy behind the music coming from this righteous mobile altar caused the tormenting spirit to leave, momentarily.

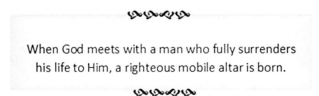

When God meets with a man who fully surrenders
his life to Him, a righteous mobile altar is born.

It saddens me when I observe much of what is called Christian worship today. It's completely void of the supernatural power of God that accompanied David's music. Many of today's leading Christian artists, seeking the fast road to fame and fortune, have sacrificed God's power in worship for entertainment. They refuse to pay the price to become musicians in the order of David — musicians who desire the anointing. To have the anointing that was on David's music, musicians must prepare themselves to pay the high spiritual price of total devotion to God. God does not testify about a lot of people. So, when He does testify, it behooves us to pay attention. God did testify that David was a man after His own heart. David was not a man after fame and fortune, even though God gave them to him. The glitz and glamour of Hollywood have seduced many Christian artists. They have become infected with the desire to become celebrities in Christendom. It is my heartfelt prayer that as God restores the "fallen tabernacle of David," that He will raise with it a new prophetic company of worship leaders in the Order of King David. *So, it came about that whenever the [evil] spirit from God was on Saul, David took a harp and played it with his hand; so, Saul would be refreshed and be well, and the evil spirit would leave him. (1 Samuel 16:23)*

In closing this section about King David and how God used him as a righteous music altar, I want you to read carefully the above Scripture, which says that every time a tormenting evil spirit came upon Saul and David played the harp, the evil spirit was cast out. It shows us that music from a righteous altar is not just to worship God, even though this is music's highest purpose. Music is also a weapon of war. Music from a higher altar triggers an immediate battle of altars. That is why if you played highly anointed worship music in a night club, there would be holy pandemonium and even riotous rage from the night club patrons. Why? Because the demons in people instinctively know when they are being confronted by the supernatural power of music emanating from a righteous altar.

Anointed Music that Shifts Atmospheres!

> *But now bring me a musician. "And it came about while the musician played, that the hand (power) of the Lord came upon Elisha. ¹⁶He said, "Thus says the Lord, 'Make this valley (the Arabah) full of trenches.' ¹⁷For thus says the Lord, 'You will not see wind or rain, yet that valley will be filled with water, so you and your cattle and your other animals may drink.*
>
> *(2 Kings 3:15-17)*

In closing, I want to draw your attention to the above passage of Scripture. This biblical story unveils another powerful dimension to the music that emanates from a righteous altar. In the story, three kings came to Elisha's prophetic chambers seeking prophetic council. One of the kings was King Ahab, the husband of the wicked woman Jezebel. The presence of King Ahab annoyed the prophet Elisha because the wickedness of this man had allowed the spirit of Jezebel to be visited on the nation of Israel. However, the presence of a righteous king by the name of Jehoshaphat saved the day. Elisha told King Ahab to come alone; Elisha would have never given him the time of day. Nevertheless, the presence of King Ahab in the room brought with it significant demonic interference in the spiritual atmosphere around the prophet. So, to cleanse the spiritual atmosphere so that his prophetic gift could function accurately, the prophet asked for an anointed minstrel to minister in music before he prophesied.

When this gifted minstrel released anointed music into the atmosphere from his righteous altar, there was an immediate shift in the spiritual climate around the prophet. Elisha's prophetic mantle got activated into high gear by worship music from a righteous altar. He began to prophesy what the three kings needed to do to turn the tide and snatch victory from the jaws of defeat. Here is what he prophesied:

> *"Thus says the Lord, 'Make this valley (the Arabah) full of trenches.' For thus says the Lord, 'You will not see wind or rain, yet that valley will be filled with*

water, so you and your cattle and your other animals may drink. This is but a simple thing in the sight of the Lord; He will also hand over the Moabites to you. You shall strike every fortified city and every choice (principal) city, and cut down every good tree and stop up all sources of water, and ruin every good piece of land with stones.'"

(2 Kings 3:17)

The following morning, when the three kings offered a sacrifice to God in response to Elisha's prophecy, water suddenly appeared [miraculously] from the area of Edom, and the country was quickly filled with water. When the Moabites looked over the valley and saw the water, they thought it was the blood of the three kings and their armies. They ran into the valley carelessly, thinking they were just going to pick up the spoils. By the time they discovered that God had tricked them, it was too late to turn back. The three kings and their armies won a decisive victory. Elisha's prophecy came to pass. This story's moral is that "anointed music" from a sanctified human attendant to a righteous altar can shift spiritual atmospheres hijacked by demons.

PRAYER OF ACTIVATION!

"Heavenly Father, I ask for the Court of Heaven to be seated and for the books of my destiny to be opened as I come before the Judge of all the earth to plead my case against any evil altar in my life or bloodline that is speaking against me. I decree and declare that the Holy Spirit is my official guide and counselor in this courtroom. Heavenly Father, I surrender all rights to self-representation; instead, I ask my defense attorney and mediator of the new covenant, the Lord Jesus Christ, to represent me in your Royal Courtroom against all idols and evil altars that are controlling my life and bloodline, in any way. I also ask the Lord Jesus to heal me by His blood from all soul wounds caused by idols and evil altars in my bloodline. I am seeking a verdict of release from the power of these evil altars in Jesus' Name.

I now enter a plea of 'guilty' into the court's records concerning any legitimate accusations that Satan has filed in Court against me or my bloodline. For Jesus said, in Matthew 5:25, "*Come to terms quickly [at the earliest opportunity] with your opponent at law while you are with him on the way [to court], so that your opponent does not hand you over to the judge, and the judge to the guard, and you are thrown into prison.*" Lord, since I am under oath, I cannot lie about my sinful activities and the iniquities of my bloodline that are connected to idolatry and the erecting evil altars. I repent for all sins and transgressions that I and my ancestors ever committed against you and the laws of nature. I repent for bowing my knees at the altar of ungodly worldly music, sung from an evil altar, in Jesus' name. Cleanse me from all sin by the blood of Jesus, according to 1 John 1:9. I now formally submit my guilty plea and repentance to the court, in Jesus' Name."

Heavenly Father,

- I decree and declare that You are destroying the evil spiritual connection between idolatry and music, in my life and bloodline, in Jesus' Name!
- I decree and declare that I am free from the spiritual consequences of my ancestors' sins, who used music to worship demons in Jesus' Name!
- I decree and declare that all opposing and evil altars against me are destroyed in Jesus' Name!
- I decree and declare that you are setting me free from all and any alter ego that Satan wants to send in my life, in Jesus' Name!
- I decree and declare that you are setting me free from idols that cause people to be physically or spiritually crippled in Jesus' Name!
- I decree and declare that I am completely healed from all soul wounds that can easily be manipulated by worldly music, in Jesus' Name!
- I decree and declare that I am building a righteous altar of music in my life and bloodline, in Jesus' Name!

LIFE APPLICATION
SECTION

Memory Verse

Whoever does not fall down and worship shall immediately be thrown into the midst of a furnace of blazing fire." [7] So when the people heard the sound of the horn, pipe, lyre, trigon, dulcimer, bagpipe and all kinds of music, all the peoples, nations, and speakers of every language fell down and worshiped the golden image that Nebuchadnezzar the king had set up.

(Daniel 3:6-7)

Reflections

1. Why are music altars so powerful?

_____

_____

_____

_____

2. What is an alter ego?

_____

_____

_____

_____

Behind every genre of music is an altar!

11

National Idols & Altars

And so Solomon finished the house (temple) of the LORD and the palace of the king. He successfully accomplished all that he had planned to do in the house of the LORD and in his palace.[12] Then the LORD appeared to Solomon by night and said to him: "I have heard your prayer and have chosen this place for Myself as a house of sacrifice.

(2 Chronicles 7:11-12)

Without a doubt, the most powerful altars (platforms) in any country are those that are officially designated as national altars. These altars, more than any other, affect the destiny of the nation. In many countries, these national altars are usually immortalized in the form of statues or monuments. When a national altar is in the form of a statue, it is usually designed to capture the likeness of a national hero the nation wishes to honor from beyond the grave. These statues (national altars) are designed to honor the life and preserve the legacy of an influential politician, freedom fighter, or national icon whose life and accomplishments were of consequence in the nation's formation.

Nevertheless, the most potent class of national altars are altars dedicated to the deity behind the nation. In the above passage of Scripture, the Bible gives us a prophetic picture of what a righteous national altar should be. After many years of the Ark of God being hosted in tents, the children of Israel, under King Solomon, finally built a magnificent temple to house the Ark of the Covenant. The dedication of this glorious temple could rival the festivities and pomp of the Oscars. After King Solomon dedicated this new home for the Ark of the Covenant, God transformed the entire building into a national altar for the nation of Israel. Consequently, Solomon's Temple became a meeting place for God's encounters with the people of Israel for many years to come. In His eternal benevolence, God told the people of Israel that this national altar (temple) would serve as a beacon of light and as a symbol of His presence. God promised that if the children of Israel did not worship other gods, He would be attentive to all the prayers that would be prayed from this national altar (Solomon's Temple).

Whether they are godly or ungodly, the purpose of national altars is to serve as a memorial to all that the deity or national hero has done for the nation in general. Some countries even create national holidays to commemorate these national altars. From my study of altars, I have concluded that some national monuments or statues are neutral; they are the nation's way of staying in touch with critical historical achievements represented by the people represented in the monument or statue.

For instance, in Washington, D.C., there are monuments and statues of President Abraham Lincoln and Reverend Martin Luther King. These monuments and statues were not erected to be worshipped by Americans as though they were gods. Unfortunately, man's propensity towards idolatry can transform a neutral national monument and statue into a spiritual stumbling block. Without a doubt, for those of us who live in the United States of America, Mount Rushmore, which contains the statues of the following presidents: George Washington, Thomas Jefferson, Abraham Lincoln, and Theodore Roosevelt, is a national altar.

The Lord told me that He had chosen Mount Rushmore to serve as a righteous altar for America to remind them of the price paid to form the greatest country on planet Earth built on Judeo-Christian values. That is why when Black Lives Matter and Antifa activists began to threaten to destroy

Mount Rushmore; I knew that this was a demonic strategy to destroy and erase America's Judeo-Christian founding. I was so blessed to see President Donald Trump make a severe stand to defend America's righteous national altar. The main-stream media called him a racist for wanting to defend the statues on Mount Rushmore. Even though the presidents who are immortalized on Mount Rushmore were not perfect men (some even owned slaves), they were nevertheless used as instruments in the hands of God to form a country that has done more for the Gospel of the Lord Jesus Christ that any other country outside of the nation of Israel.

Idolatrous National Altars

> *Then the Philistines took the ark of God, and they brought it from Ebenezer to Ashdod. ² They took the ark of God and brought it into the house of Dagon and set it beside [the image of] Dagon [their chief idol].*
>
> *(1 Samuel 5:1-2)*

Unfortunately, ever since the fall of Adam and Eve in the Garden of Eden, man's propensity towards idolatry and the erecting of evil altars is unmatched by any other species. Just as there are righteous or spiritually neutral national altars, there are also demonically engineered national altars built by spiritual or political leaders whose heart is full of idolatry. These evil national altars are spiritual in every way. They are designed to ensnare the souls of men into worshipping Satan. In the above passage of Scripture from the book of 1 Samuel, the Bible tells us that when the Philistines captured the Ark of God, they took it to the temple of Dagon. The Bible identifies Dagon as the national idol of the Philistines, which means that the temple he was housed in was the national altar of Philistia. It did not take long before there was a spiritual confrontation between the Ark of God and the Philistines' demonic national altar. I believe much of the religious and politically motivated violence in most nations is due to the battle of altars that ensues between righteous citizens in the country and those who want their country to bow down to Satan. Understanding the subject of altars is critical to rescuing the destiny of nations from Satan's grip.

Religious and politically motivated conflicts in a
nation are really a battle of altars.

The Evil National Altar of Planned Parenthood

*You shall not give any of your children to offer them [by fire as a sacrifice] to
Molech [the god of the Ammonites], nor shall you profane the name of your
God [by honoring idols as gods]. I am the LORD.*

Leviticus 18:21

As a black man living in America, I used to think that America's greatest
sin is its past was the enslavement of people of color. I believed this until the
day the Holy Spirit disagreed with me. He said to me, "Francis, while slavery
was atrocious, fewer black people were killed during slavery than the millions
of black babies that have been aborted since Roe V. Wade became established
law in America." It suddenly dawned on me that since this demonic law became
the law of the land, over 61 million babies have been aborted in America. That
is a staggering number by any stretch of the imagination. Of that number, over
43% is the number of African American babies murdered in their mother's
womb at the altar of a woman's right to choose.

According to the above passage of Scripture, the demonic deity closely
associated with child sacrifice was Molech. In several instances in the Bible,
God sternly forbids the children of Israel from participating in the worship
of Molech by sacrificing their children to this abomination. In the United
States of America, the number one guardian of Molech's altar is a powerful
organization called Planned Parenthood. This organization was founded by
Margaret Sanger, who was an avowed eugenist. She was a well-known racist
who hated black people and wanted to slow down their ability to procreate. She
founded Planned Parenthood for that specific purpose under the euphemism
of giving women a voice in family planning. The only problem is that the
modality of family planning she chose was the sacrificing (abortion) of
children at Molech's altar.

Whether the employees of Planned Parenthood know it or not, they are human attendants to the altar of Molech, and they have a lot of innocent blood on their hands. If you listen to the Democratic Party, it is clear that they see Planned Parenthood as a national altar of America and violently protect it. There is no way to sugar coat this; Christians who say they follow Jesus, who vote for a political platform that is this passionately addicted to defending the altar of Molech, are just as guilty of endorsing this demonic practice as the abortion doctor and nurse who perform these merciless abortions.

Kingdom Citizens need to know that their vote has a voice in the Courts of Heaven. What you vote for, you also cosign for. In the banking world, a cosigner accepts the responsibility of the debt and is held liable when the actual owner of the loan defaults. I am not suggesting that Christians who vote for the Democratic Party are going to hell; that is between them and God. However, at the very least, their hands are smeared with the blood of the unborn that Planned Parenthood, with the support of the Democratic Party, willfully abort. Have you noticed that very few Planned Parenthood clinics, if any, are found in rich and upper-class white neighborhoods? However, these facilities are in abundance in Black and Hispanic neighborhoods. The message is loud and clear. The agenda of Margaret Sanger, to exterminate races of people she thought were inferior, never died with her. Under the euphemism of promoting a woman's right to do with her body as she pleases, her organization has successfully managed to recruit the passionate support of the very race of people (Blacks) that Margaret Sanger was determined to exterminate.

Thankfully, God has shown me that the *witchcraft of identity politics* that the Democratic Party perpetuates on African Americans to exploit Black pain is collapsing. There is a prophetic generation of African Americans who God is raising who will not exchange the abortion of Black babies for political platitudes on race and social justice. Imagine how formidable a voting bloc of African Americans would have been if we had kept all 20 million-plus of the babies we have aborted? I can only imagine! May God judge and destroy this demonic national altar of abortion, which has ensnared Americans for generations. Whatever your opinion on President Donald Trump, he has been determined to be the most pro-life president America has ever had. In the grand scheme of things, I know that God is less concerned about a stupid tweet by President Trump than He is about the instrument of death the abortion doctor uses to extract the life of an innocent and defenseless baby, who feels pain! Jesus help us and have mercy on our souls – *no allegiance to a Political Party can be this important!*

> Planned Parenthood & its employees, are attendants to the altar of Molech!

Prayer of Activation!

Courts of Heaven:
Divorce Decree from Baal & Molech

"Heavenly Father, Righteous Judge, I ask for the Court of Heaven to be seated, as I come before the Judge of all the earth to plead my case so I can be justified and acquitted of all charges related to idolatry or the erecting of evil altars in my bloodline. Heavenly Father, I am here in the courtroom with my official representative, the Holy Spirit, my advocate, and counselor. Heavenly Father, I surrender all rights to self-representation. Instead, I ask my defense attorney and mediator of the new covenant, the Lord Jesus Christ, to represent me in your Royal courtroom as I seek a bill of divorcement from Baal and Molech.

Heavenly Father, Righteous Judge, I now enter a plea of 'guilty' into the court's records concerning anything I have in common in my soul or bloodline with the worship of Baal and Molech, in Jesus name, I pray. The Bible says in Matthew 5:25, *Agree with thine adversary quickly, whiles thou art in the way with him; lest at any time the adversary deliver thee to the judge, and the judge deliver thee to the officer, and thou be cast into prison.* Lord, since I am under oath I cannot lie about my sinful activities and the iniquities of my bloodline that are connected to idolatry, especially any marriage with the altars of Baal and Molech. So, I agree with any legitimate accusations brought by Satan against me and my bloodline. I now repent of all sins of idolatry and the erecting of evil altars to Baal and Molech in my soul or that my ancestors ever committed. LORD it is written in 1 John 1:9, *"If we [freely] admit that we have sinned and confess our sins, He is faithful and just [true to His own nature and promises], and will forgive our sins and cleanse us continually from all unrighteousness [our wrongdoing, everything not in conformity with His will and purpose]."*

Heavenly Father, Righteous Judge, I now ask Your Court to grant me an irrevocable 'Bill of Divorcement' from Baal and Molech, based upon the following Scripture, 2 Corinthians 6:14-17, *"Do not be unequally bound together with unbelievers [do not make mismatched alliances with them, inconsistent with your faith]. For what partnership can righteousness have with lawlessness? Or what fellowship can light have with darkness? 15 What harmony can there be between Christ and Belial (Satan)? Or what does a believer have in common with an unbeliever? 16 What agreement is there between the temple of God and idols? For we are the temple of the living God; just as God said: "I will dwell among them and walk among them; And I will be their God, and they shall be My people. 17 "So come out from among unbelievers and be separate," says the Lord, "And do not touch what is unclean; And I will graciously receive you and welcome you [with favor].*

Based on the above Scripture, I ask for a Bill of Divorcement in Jesus' mighty name.

FINAL DECREE OF DIVORCE

The Court of Heaven finds that the parties have entered into a fully enforceable written agreement as contained in this decree, having approved this decree both in form and substance. To the extent permitted by the laws of the Kingdom of Heaven, the parties stipulate the agreement is enforceable as a contract recognized by this Court. The Court of Heaven approves the agreement of the parties as contained in this Final Decree of Divorce.

IT IS HEREBY ORDERED AND DECREED

that _____ (insert your name), Petitioner, and Baal and Molech, Respondents, are divorced and that the marriage between them is dissolved on the grounds of incompatibility and violation of the First Commandment. This Bill of Divorcement is henceforth decreed and sealed in the Blood of the Savior, Jesus Christ of Nazareth.

Signature:_____Date:_____

LIFE APPLICATION

SECTION

Memory Verse

You shall not give any of your children to offer them [by fire as a sacrifice] to Molech [the god of the Ammonites], nor shall you profane the name of your God [by honoring idols as gods]. I am the LORD.

(Leviticus 18:21)

Reflections

1. What is a national altar?

   _____

   _____

   _____

   _____

2. Why is Planned Parenthood an attendant to the altar of Molech?

   _____

   _____

   _____

   _____

12

The Cross: The Highest Altar on Earth

Then he handed Him over to them to be crucified. [17]So they took Jesus, and He went out, bearing His own cross, to the place called the Place of the Skull, which is called in Hebrew, Golgotha. [18]There they crucified Him, and with Him two others, one on either side, and Jesus between them.

(John 19:16-18)

Without any contradiction, the Cross of Christ on which Jesus was crucified is absolutely the highest altar on earth. When Pontius Pilate handed Him over to the Roman soldiers to be crucified, he unwittingly changed the course of human history, and the time continuum was split into two frames, B.C. and A.D.

B.C. (Before Christ) speaks to the time on earth that covers the creation of Adam, his tragic fall into a life of sin and death, and everything that has since followed this unfortunate event before Christ arrived on our troubled planet.

A.D (Anno Domini, in the year of our Lord) speaks to the time when the trajectory of the fall of mankind and Satan's reign on earth were divinely intercepted by the Nazarene. The Nazarene is Jesus the Messiah who was born in a manger and was eventually crucified on an instrument of torture designed by the Romans called "the cross." A.D represents this prophetic period of grace the Bible calls the New Covenant! During this dispensation of grace, everyone who bows their knees in repentance at the foot of the cross, no matter their sin, can find God's redemptive grace to become children of God. At the foot of the Cross of Christ, all men can be reconciled to God. Such is the incredible power of the altar of the Cross of Christ.

Some of you reading this book may not have considered the fact that the Cross of Christ is an altar. The truth of the matter is that it functions precisely as an altar. The Cross of Christ carries the following features of an altar:

- It's a place where divinity can meet with humanity. That is what happens when a person comes to the saving knowledge of Jesus Christ, and their sins are cleansed by the blood of the cross.
- It's a place of divine exchange where we exchange our sinful condition for the righteousness of the Son of God. That is what Paul meant in 2 Corinthians 5:21 when he said, *"He has made Him to be sin who did not know sin that we might become the righteousness of God in Christ Jesus."*
- Like any altar, the cross is fueled by the sacrifice made by its human attendant; in this case, the Lord Jesus Christ gave Himself as the sacrifice as an appropriation for our sin.
- Like any altar, the cross is the place where God cut the "covenant of grace with mankind," and it's also where He sustains it.

So, by any stretch of the imagination or theological analysis, the Cross of Jesus Christ bears all the marks of an altar and much more!

The Cross: An Altar of Consecration & Healing

He personally carried our sins in His body on the [a]cross [willingly offering Himself on it, as on an altar of sacrifice], so that we might die to sin [becoming

immune from the penalty and power of sin] and live for righteousness; for by
His wounds you [who believe] have been healed.

(1 Peter 2:24)

In his epistle, Peter the Apostle lets us know that the altar of the Cross of Christ is an altar of consecration and healing. He makes it abundantly clear that at the Cross, Jesus personally took our sin in His body, and the reason He did this is so that we may die to sin.

It's very interesting how this passage of Scripture is light years ahead of modern science and medicine in the making of a vaccine. When medical doctors and scientists create a vaccine, the protocol they use is very similar to what the Apostle Peter is describing in the above passage of Scripture. In making a vaccine, scientists take a healthy tissue and expose it to the virus they're trying to eliminate. Once the healthy tissue builds up immunity against the virus, it builds up what is known as "antibodies." The healthy tissue is then culturized into a medicine. The medicine created from exposing the healthy tissue to the virus is then used as a vaccine used to inoculate people to avoid being infected by the virus.

That is just what God did with Jesus. Since the fall of Adam and Eve, mankind has been under a pandemic of sin that has distorted our God-given DNA and the divine nature of God within us. So, a spiritual vaccine was needed to inoculate all of mankind against the "virus of Sin." On the Cross, God exposed Jesus, the healthy tissue, to every sin known or unknown to man. Thanks be to God, Jesus prevailed. Consequently, the blood of Jesus contains all the "divine antibodies" we need to be cured of Sin's virus and the sinful nature it has created in our souls. We can now come to the author of the altar of the cross of Christ and exchange our sinful nature for His divine nature. Glory to God!

Once scientists finish culturizing a medication created from exposing healthy tissue to the virus they were trying to cure – a vaccine is created! This vaccine is then injected intravenously into the bloodstreams of the population. In most cases, the vaccine has the desired effect of creating antibodies in the bloodstream that immunizes the person from contracting the virus. That is precisely what God did with the spiritual medication He created by exposing Jesus to Sin's virus on the Cross. Therefore, the blood Jesus shed from the Cross contains the spiritual antibodies we need to be healed from every disease and sickness known to man resulting from sin. It is no wonder the Apostle Peter says, "by His stripes, you were healed" making the altar of the Cross of Christ an instrument of physical healing. It is impossible to underestimate the healing potentials of the Cross of Christ.

The Cross: An Altar of Self Denial

Then Jesus said to His disciples, "If anyone wishes to follow Me [as My disciple], he must deny himself [set aside selfish interests], and take up his cross [expressing a willingness to endure whatever may come] and follow Me [believing in Me, conforming to My example in living and, if need be, suffering or perhaps dying because of faith in Me]. ²⁵*For whoever wishes to save his life [in this world] will [eventually] lose it [through death], but whoever loses his life [in this world] for My sake will find it [that is, life with Me for all eternity].* ²⁶*For what will it profit a man if he gains the whole world [wealth, fame, success], but forfeits his soul? Or what will a man give in exchange for his soul?*

(Matthew 16:24-26)

God divinely inspires every Scripture, but no word in the Bible is weightier than the words spoken directly from the mouth of God. In the New Testament, Bible translators went out of their way to highlight all the words of Jesus in red. It is clear no one understood the importance of the altar of the Cross as clearly as the person who would later give His life on it! Jesus informed all of His disciples then, and now, that no one can become an effective disciple of Jesus who is not tied to the altar of the Cross. Most important, Jesus let us know that the altar of the Cross is an altar of self-denial. Here is what Jesus said in the Amplified Version of the Bible,

ᔆᔆᔆᔆ

The cross of Christ is the place where divinity met humanity, where a divine exchange took place, it was fueled by human sacrifice, and where God "cut" the Covenant.

ᔆᔆᔆᔆ

If anyone wishes to follow Me [as My disciple], he must deny himself [set aside selfish interests], and take up his cross [expressing a willingness to endure whatever may come] and follow Me [believing in Me, conforming to My example in living and, if need be, suffering or perhaps dying because of faith in Me].

(Matthew 16:24)

There is no sugar-coating this. Jesus boldly announced the cost of true discipleship. God invested in the altar of the Cross of Christ the ability to inscribe a spirit of self-denial upon man's self-centered heart. Let's be honest: left to our own devices, we are selfish beings controlled by our selfish interests and desires. Unfortunately, all our carnal desires bring us into enmity with God and His way of doing things. In His creative genius, God designed the perfect instrument of circumcision: the Cross of Christ! The current widespread immorality in the Church stands as a witness to the lack of self-consecration and self-denial in the Body of Christ. That is a severe indictment against the user-friendly and seeker-sensitive messages that are coming out of many churches. I hear God saying, "Bring back the Cross!"

Bring Back the Message of the Cross!

For the message of the cross is foolishness [absurd and illogical] to those who are perishing and spiritually dead [because they reject it], but to us who are being saved [by God's grace] it is [the manifestation of] the power of God.

(1 Corinthians 1:18)

The Holy Spirit wants spiritual leaders in the Body of Christ to bring back the message of the Cross! The Apostle Paul, in the book of First Corinthians, unravels the mystery behind the reason most seeker-sensitive churches do not preach the message of the Cross. Paul says the message of the Cross is foolish, absurd, and illogical to those who are perishing and spiritually dead. This explains why so many carnally minded Christians reject the message of the Cross. They call the preaching of the Cross legalism.

Consequently, in disdain, they reject the message of the Cross in the name of the doctrine of grace. They say, "We are not under the Law; we are under grace." The irony is that there would be no grace for us to access without the Cross of Christ. It is the Cross of Christ that purchased our access to the throne of grace! Jesus' sacrificial death on the Cross transformed God's judicial seat of judgment into a throne of grace and mercy. Consequently, when we reject the altar of the Cross of Christ, we, in essence, forfeit the grace of God that was purchased for us by the "One" who gave His life for us on the Cross. That is why we desperately need to bring back to the Church the message of the Cross.

The Cross: An Altar that Answers the Law

…having canceled out the certificate of debt consisting of legal demands [which were in force] against us and which were hostile to us. And this certificate He has set aside and completely removed by nailing it to the cross.

(Colossians 2:14)

The Apostle Paul, the author of the Book of Colossians, goes a step further in unveiling for us the power of the altar of the Cross of Christ. He boldly declared, "The Lord Jesus Christ canceled out the 'certificate of debt' that we had sitting on top of our heads consisting of the legal demands of the Law of Moses, which were in force against us." The million-dollar question is, "What is the certificate of debt that the Apostle Paul is alluding to?" According to Paul, we were unable to pay this certificate of debt, and it was actually "… hostile to our fallen nature." The expression "hostile to…" in the biblical passage implies that our fallen nature is incapable of complying with God's righteous law. Everything in man's sinful nature is primed to rebel against the authority of God. Romans 5:13-14 gives us a glimpse into what is responsible for the certificate of debt that we owed God by virtue of our sinful nature:

> *Sin was [committed] in the world before the Law [was given], but sin is not charged [against anyone] when there is no law [against it].* [14]*Yet death ruled [over mankind] from Adam to Moses [the Lawgiver], even over those who had not sinned [a]as Adam did. Adam is a type of Him (Christ) who was to come [but in reverse—Adam brought destruction, Christ brought salvation].*
>
> *(Romans 5:13-14)*

According to Romans 5:13-14, sin was in the world operating through man's fallen nature, long before the law of Moses was given in written text on tablets of stone, which showed us that sin is a transgression of the law of God. However, according to this Scripture passage, sin is not charged against anyone when there's no law against it! Unfortunately for us, God's law is retroactive! Consequently, as soon as God instituted the Law of Moses on Mount Sinai, all men became guilty of every transgression that they'd ever committed on this planet since the fall of Adam and Eve. So, God filed all of these offenses of mankind into one universal certificate for debt that Paul refers to as a "certificate of debt of legal demands of the law," which were in force against us. Can you imagine living in a house for many years "rent-free" only to receive in the mail, one fateful day, a "certificate of debt" from the bank for all the years you've lived in a house that you thought was rent-free?

That would be terrifying to anybody and is precisely what happened in the Old Covenant when God gave the Law to Moses on Mount Sinai. Finally and dutifully, "all charges" against sins past and present could now be leveled against the entire human race. So, thousands of years of man's fallen nature was now filed against the human race in the Courts of Heaven. Over many generations, "sin's debt" kept accumulating with interest, year after year. This certificate of debt also gave Satan, the arch-enemy of our souls, the legal right to drag the souls of men into eternal damnation if they died before repenting to God for their sins. Thankfully, in the most romantic story of love ever told, Jesus, the perfect man, gave Himself on the altar of the Cross to pay this insurmountable certificate of debt that mankind had collectively accumulated. In offering His life in total of obedience to God, He paid the full penalty of the law of Moses, which demanded uncompromisingly that "the sinner must die" for his or her sin! That is why Jesus died for the "sin" of all of us on the altar of the Cross. Glory be God in the Highest!

The Cross: An Altar of Triumph over Demonic Principalities!

> *When He had disarmed the rulers and authorities [those supernatural forces of evil operating against us], He made a public example of them [exhibiting them as captives in His triumphal procession], having triumphed over them through] the cross.*
>
> *(Colossians 2:15)*

The Apostle Paul goes another step further in bragging about the tremendous power of the altar of the Cross when he boldly declares that at the Cross, Jesus our Lord, disarmed supernatural forces of evil — the rulers and authorities of this present world of darkness. These demonic principalities, with Satan leading the charge, were operating against us! According to the Apostle Paul, Jesus made a public spectacle of these demonic principalities by triumphing over them on the Cross. According to the Apostle Paul, Jesus not only nailed sin to the Cross, He also disarmed Satan and his minions who depend on the sins of men to drag the souls of men to hell.

It is the transgressing of the Law of God that gives Satan the legal right to bind, kill, and destroy men's souls. In nailing sin to the Cross, Jesus effectively pulled Satan's rug from under him by abolishing the thing that gave him the legal right to the souls of men. This is why, under the New Testament's dispensation of grace, people are no longer going to hell because of sin. They end up in hell for rejecting the one, Jesus of Nazareth, who paid the price for their sins on the altar of the Cross.

Each time we teach on the altar of the Cross of Christ, we actually reinforce Christ's disarmament of demonic principalities and powers in heavenly places.

That is why pastors and apostolic leaders in the Body of Christ must teach the message of the Cross! Satan fears this glorious message.

The Altar of the Cross & the Supernatural Power of God

And when I came to you, brothers and sisters, proclaiming to you the testimony of God [concerning salvation through Christ], I did not come with superiority of speech or of wisdom [no lofty words of eloquence or of philosophy as a Greek orator might do]; ²for I made the decision to know nothing [that is, to forego philosophical or theological discussions regarding inconsequential things and opinions while] among you except Jesus Christ, and Him crucified [and the meaning of His redemptive, substitutionary death and His resurrection]. ³I came to you in [a state of] weakness and fear and great trembling. ⁴And my message and my preaching were not in persuasive words of wisdom [using clever rhetoric], but [they were delivered] in demonstration of the [Holy] Spirit [operating through me] and of [His] power [stirring the minds of the listeners and persuading them],

(1 Corinthians 2:1-4)

In 1 Corinthians, the Apostle Paul finally connects the message of the altar of the Cross of Christ to the release of the supernatural power of God. He makes it very clear that for believers in Christ to operate in the supernatural power of God, we must be found standing on the altar of the Cross. Here is how the Apostle Paul described the attitude he had when he came to preach to the Corinthians:

> *When I came to you, brothers and sisters, proclaiming to you the testimony of God [concerning salvation through Christ], I did not come with superiority of speech or of wisdom [no lofty words of eloquence or of philosophy as a Greek orator might do]; for I made the decision to know nothing [that is, to forego philosophical or theological discussions regarding inconsequential things and opinions while] among you except Jesus Christ, and Him crucified [and the meaning of His redemptive, substitutionary death and His resurrection].*
>
> *(1 Corinthians 2:1-2)*

Apostle Paul makes it very clear that we cannot preach the Kingdom's message using the superiority of speech, or human wisdom, or philosophy as a Greek orator might do. Not wanting to take away from the superiority of the altar of the Cross of Christ, even though he was very educated, he made a conscious decision not to pull on his understanding of philosophy or theology to discuss what Jesus Christ did for mankind. Instead, he relied completely on the awesome power of what Christ did on the altar of the Cross when He gave His life for all mankind. Paul goes on to say,

> *My message and my preaching were not in persuasive words of wisdom [using clever rhetoric], but [they were delivered] in demonstration of the [Holy] Spirit [operating through me] and of [His] power [stirring the minds of the listeners and persuading them].*
>
> *(1 Corinthians 2:4)*

What Paul is saying here is obvious. You don't have to be a rocket scientist to figure it out. The supernatural demonstration of the Holy Spirit's power in miracles, signs, and wonders in the New Testament is directly connected to the preaching of the message of the Cross. No wonder Satan doesn't want the Church to dwell on the message of the Cross of Christ! He wants us to teach "feel good" messages such as *Five Steps to a New You.*" Satan doesn't mind us doing this, provided we never teach on the incredible power of the altar of the Cross. I believe that each time we teach on the altar of the Cross of Christ, we reinforce Christ's disarmament of these demonic principalities and powers in heavenly places. Consequently, we also reinforce our own spiritual authority in Christ Jesus over these demonic principalities.

It is Finished!

> After this, Jesus, knowing that all was now finished, said in fulfillment of the Scripture, "I am thirsty." ²⁹A jar full of sour wine was placed there; so they put a sponge soaked in the sour wine on [a branch of] hyssop and held it to His mouth. ³⁰When Jesus had received the sour wine, He said, "It is finished!" And He bowed His head and [voluntarily] gave up His spirit.
>
> (John 19:28-30)

The final and most memorable thing the Lord Jesus Christ did on the altar of the Cross to consummate His victory over sin, death, hell, and the grave is to declare, "It is finished!" These words, "It is finished," rang like a piercing trumpet blast through the corridors of hell.

These words, 'It is finished,' echoed like a Shofar through all the multiple dimensions of the Heavenly Kingdom. Mankind had finally been redeemed! The certificate of debt of past and future transgressions had been paid-in-full! These words, 'It is finished,' made the altar of the Cross the ultimate and primary custodian of the 'finished work' of the Messiah!

In other words, no man could talk about the "finished work" of the man Christ Jesus separate from glorying in the cross upon which He sacrificed His life as an atonement for sin. That is why when we stand on the altar of the cross and fully identify with it in our daily walk as we carry the cross through a life of self-denial, Satan literally has zero authority in our lives. Glory to God in the highest!

࿇࿇࿇࿇࿇

Man was given territorial and stewardship authority over the planet Earth.

࿇࿇࿇࿇࿇

PRAYER OF ACTIVATION!

"Heavenly Father, I ask for the Court of Heaven to be seated and for the books of my destiny to be opened as I come before the Judge of all the earth to plead my case against any evil altar in my life or bloodline that is speaking against me. I decree and declare that the Holy Spirit is my official guide and counselor in this courtroom. Heavenly Father, I surrender all rights to self-representation; instead, I ask my defense attorney and mediator of the new covenant, the Lord Jesus Christ, to represent me in your Royal Courtroom against all idols and evil altars that are controlling my life and bloodline, in any way. I also ask the Lord Jesus to heal me by His blood from all soul wounds caused by idols and evil altars in my bloodline. I am seeking a verdict of release from the power of these evil altars in Jesus' Name.

I now enter a plea of 'guilty' into the court's records concerning any legitimate accusations that Satan has filed in Court against me or my bloodline. For Jesus said, in Matthew 5:25, *"Come to terms quickly [at the earliest opportunity] with your opponent at law while you are with him on the way [to court], so that your opponent does not hand you over to the judge, and the judge to the guard, and you are thrown into prison."* Lord, since I am under oath, I cannot lie about my sinful activities and the iniquities of my bloodline that are connected to idolatry and the erecting evil altars. I repent for all sins and transgressions that I and my ancestors ever committed against you and the laws of nature. I repent for times I have failed to carry my cross as Jesus commanded all of His disciples to do. Cleanse me from all sin by the blood of Jesus, according to 1 John 1:9. I now formally submit my guilty plea and repentance to the court, in Jesus' Name."

Heavenly Father,

- I decree and declare that the altar of the Cross of Christ sets me free from the seducing power of Sin, in Jesus' Name!
- I decree and declare that every evil altar which is speaking is silenced by the power of the altar of the Cross of Christ, in Jesus' Name!
- I decree and declare that I have already secured total victory against any spirit of disease or infirmity because of the Cause of Christ, in Jesus' Name!
- I decree and declare that altar of the Cross of Christ releases upon me a spirit of self-denial and sacrifice in Jesus' Name!
- I decree and declare that the altar of the Cross of Christ silences every altar of tradition and legalism in my life or bloodline in Jesus' Name!
- I decree and declare that I am completely healed from all soul wounds because of the finished work of Jesus on the Cross, in Jesus' Name!
- I decree and declare that I am a victor in the battle of altars through the power of the Cross of Christ, in Jesus' Name!

LIFE APPLICATION

SECTION

Memory Verse

He personally carried our sins in His body on the [a]cross [willingly offering Himself on it, as on an altar of sacrifice], so that we might die to sin [becoming immune from the penalty and power of sin] and live for righteousness; for by His wounds you [who believe] have been healed.

(1 Peter 2:24)

Reflections

1. Why is the Cross of Christ referred to as altar?

    _____

    _____

    _____

    _____

2. Name two divine exchanges, which transpire when humans bend their knees at the altar of the Cross of Christ?

    _____

    _____

    _____

    _____

Miracles are connected to altars!

13

The Altar of Melchizedek: The Highest Altar in all of Creation

We have an altar from which those who serve and [worship in the tabernacle have no right to eat. ¹¹For when the blood of animals is brought into the sanctuary by the high priest as a sacrifice for sin, the victims' bodies are burned outside the limits of the camp. ¹²Therefore Jesus also suffered and died outside the [city's] gate in order that He might purify and consecrate the people through [the shedding of] His own blood and set them apart as holy [for God].

(Hebrews 13:10-12)

In the above passage of Scripture, the writer of the Book of Hebrews tells us that we have an altar from which those who serve and worship in the tabernacle have "no right to eat." What is he talking about? The tabernacle in the text refers to the Tabernacle of Moses that was stewarded by the Levi priesthood.

The priesthood of Levi was an earthly priesthood that God instituted in the nation of Israel to foreshadow its higher heavenly counterpart, the Order of Melchizedek! In this final chapter on the battle of altars, we will conclude this powerful revelation by unveiling the highest altar in all of creation. This is the altar that the writer of Hebrews is referencing in the above passage of Scripture.

In Bible college, there is a principle of hermeneutics taught in the art of interpreting Scripture. This principle is called the "principle of first mention." According to this principle, the first time a subject is mentioned in the Bible carries the "highest meaning and proper application" of that subject throughout the entirety of the body of Scripture. Following this principle, the first time the word "priest" is ever mentioned has to do with Melchizedek's appearance when he intercepted Abraham in the Valley of Kings.

> *Melchizedek, King of Salem (ancient Jerusalem), brought out bread and wine [for them]; he was the priest of God Most High. And Melchizedek blessed Abram and said, "Blessed (joyful, favored) be Abram by God Most High, Creator and Possessor of heaven and earth. And blessed, praised, and glorified be God Most High, Who has given your enemies into your hand." And Abram gave him a tenth of all [the treasure he had taken in battle].*
>
> *(Genesis 14:18-20)*

The second time that the word "priest" is mentioned in the Bible is in Genesis 41:45, describing the Egyptian priesthood of "Oni," which was actually a demonic priesthood that serviced all the gods of Egypt. This reference to the priesthood of "Oni" is a clear indication that Satan, the master copycat, wasted no time mimicking the spiritual technology behind the priesthood God established. Satan wanted a lineage of people on earth who could provide him with a confederacy of false priesthoods that could erect evil altars to Satan.

After Moses received the Law on Mount Sinai, the Lord commanded Moses to consecrate the tribe of Levi to become priests in Israel. They would effectively become human attendants to the altar of God within the nation of Israel. Nevertheless, whichever way you slice it, the first priesthood mentioned in the Bible is the priesthood of Melchizedek, which lets us know that God judges the suitability of any priesthood by comparing it to how closely it resembles the heavenly priesthood of Melchizedek. Since the primary function of the priesthood of God is to attend to His altar, the question becomes, 'What are the spiritual dynamics of the altar of Melchizedek, and where is this superior altar located?' These questions will be answered in this chapter. For more information on the Order of Melchizedek, please read my book, *The Order of Melchizedek*.

A Perfecting Altar!

> *Now if perfection [a perfect fellowship between God and the worshiper] had been attained through the Levitical priesthood (for under it the people were given the Law) what further need was there for another and different kind of priest to arise, one in the manner of Melchizedek, rather than one appointed to the order of Aaron? *[12]*For when there is a change in the priesthood, there is of necessity a change of the law [concerning the priesthood] as well. *[13]*For the One of whom these things are said belonged [not to the priestly line of Levi but] to another tribe, from which no one has officiated or served at the altar.*
>
> (Hebrews 7:11-13)

One of the first things the writer of the Book of Hebrews tells us about the altar of Melchizedek is that it is a "perfecting altar." The writer of the Book of Hebrews makes the argument that "if perfection" (that is establishing a perfect relationship between God and man) could be attained through the Levitical priesthood, God would have done it. There would have been no need for another priest to arise after the manner and Order of Melchizedek, such as the Lord Jesus Christ. Under the Levitical priesthood, the children of Israel received the Law of God. However, after 4000 years since the fall of Adam and Eve, it was clear that man's fallen nature was incapable of keeping the Law of God. Consequently, another system of perfecting man's fellowship with God was needed. According to the author of Hebrews, not only was a new system of perfecting man's fellowship with God needed, a completely different and higher priesthood with a human attendant, who did not have the same idiosyncrasies as the high priests of the tribe of Levi, was needed.

So, when the Lord Jesus showed up on the earth, originating from the tribe of Judah, began to function as a priest, it was very unusual because Moses had said nothing about a priesthood of God to come from the tribe of Judah. Only the tribe of Levi had been selected for the priesthood. Consequently, whatever "priesthood" Jesus Christ was functioning in; it was not the priesthood of Levi. Like King David before Him, who was also from the tribe of Judah, the Lord was functioning in a higher priestly order. To my knowledge, the only righteous priestly order that was ever revealed to the children of Israel apart from the priesthood of Levi is the priesthood of Melchizedek. That means that when Jesus was functioning as a priest on earth, he was doing it under the Order of Melchizedek. It also means that the Lord Jesus was an "attendant" to a "different type of altar" than that of the tribe of Levi. That is why priests from the tribe of Levi had no right to eat from the altar of Melchizedek. They had their own earthly altar. What cannot be argued is that the writer of the Book of Hebrews connects the altar Jesus attends to, to the whole subject of perfecting the relationship between God and man. When we align ourselves with the Altar of Melchizedek in heaven, our relationship with God begins to get perfected in both spiritual sensitivity and maturity.

〰〰〰〰

The blood, as a substance for giving life, is very unique to every organ we have in our body because the blood, unlike the other organs of our body, did not originate on earth.

〰〰〰〰

The Altar of Melchizedek: the Altar of the Slain Lamb

All who dwell on the earth will worship him, whose names have not been written in the Book of Life of the Lamb slain from the foundation of the world.

(Revelation 13:8, NKJV)

In the above passage of Scripture, Saint John, the revelator, is shown a life-changing mystery. The Lord showed him the Book of Life, sealed in the "blood of the Lamb," the lamb that was slain by God Himself before the foundation of the world. First and foremost, this means that the blood, as a substance for giving life, is unique to every organ we have in our body. That is because the blood, unlike our body's other organs, did not originate on earth. It originated from the realms of eternity! However, the above passage of Scripture begs the question, "If Jesus is the Lamb of God slain before the foundation of the world, at what altar was this?" That is important because the slaying of a lamb as a sacrificial offering to God can only happen at an altar. So, what altar is this that is already positioned in the heavenly kingdom, long before the world began? From my extensive study of the subject of Melchizedek, I am more than convinced that the altar of the slain Lamb is the altar of Melchizedek that is in heaven! It is no wonder Moses was admonished by God to build the tabernacle according to the pattern of the tabernacle in heaven.

The Blood of the Altar of Melchizedek

But you have come to Mount Zion and to the city of the living God, the heavenly Jerusalem, to an innumerable company of angels, [23]to the [a]general assembly and church of the firstborn who are registered in heaven, to God the Judge of all, to the spirits of just men made perfect, [24]to Jesus the Mediator of the new covenant, and to the blood of sprinkling that speaks better things than that of Abel.

(Hebrews 12:22-24)

The writer of the Book of Hebrews tells us that as believers in Christ, through our union with Jesus, we have come into a dimension of living on Mount Zion, the city of the living God. Here are some attributes of Mount Zion.

- It is the spiritual location of the heavenly Jerusalem that will one day come down from heaven to the earth so that the abode of God will be with men forever and ever, Amen.
- Mount Zion is where we can access an innumerable company of angels of different orders, sizes, and rankings.

- Mount Zion is the spiritual location of the General Assembly and Church of the Firstborn, whose names are registered in heaven in the Lamb's Book of Life.
- Mount Zion is also the spiritual location of the dimension known as the "Courts of Heaven," a place of judicial activity for executing God's righteous judgments here on the earth.

However, I want to draw your attention to Hebrews 12:24, which seems to suggest the presence of an altar – a living altar in heaven very powerfully.

In a previous chapter, I told you about the laws of altars. Every altar requires a human attendant, and all altars are places of covenant. Additionally, every altar is fueled or powered by the sacrifice or offering of its human attendant.

In Hebrews 12:24, we clearly see that Jesus is an attendant to an altar that maintains and sustains the new covenant. Most important, the altar is sprinkled with His precious blood. It is also clear from the unfolding revelation on altars in Scripture that the highest offering a human attendant can give to an altar is blood. That is why the cultural fight in America over abortion rights has little to do with the question of a woman's right to choose. It's all about Satan refusing to let go of an institution (Planned Parenthood) that supplies him and his demonic kingdom with an endless supply of the blood of innocent babies. It is also why many people in the occult drink human blood to gain strength and spiritual power. The altar of Melchizedek in heaven is where we find the blood of the Lamb, who is Jesus Christ of Nazareth. Hallelujah!

The Priesthood of Zion

The Lord said to my Lord, "Sit at My right hand, Till I make Your enemies Your footstool." ²The Lord shall send the rod of Your strength out of Zion. Rule in the midst of Your enemies! ⁴The Lord has sworn and will not relent, "You are a priest forever according to the order of Melchizedek."

(Psalm 110:1-2, 4)

King David, in the above passage of Scripture, makes it very clear that the Order of Melchizedek is the priesthood of Zion. I have already shown you in Hebrews 12:22 that Mount Zion is the city of the living God. Mount Zion is not an earthly city. It's a heavenly city of God. It's a city of angels and the redeemed of the Lord. King David had a life-changing prophetic encounter that would mark him for the rest of his life. In this prophetic vision, the Lord showed him something spectacular. He saw the heavenly Father speaking to the second member of the Godhead, the man we know as Jesus, thousands of years before He became the incarnate son of God on earth. This is what God said to the Messiah: *"Sit at My right hand till I make Your enemies Your footstool. The Lord shall send the rod of Your strength out of Zion. Rule in the midst of Your enemies."* (Psalm 110:2) The only person in Scripture the Bible says is seated at the right hand of God the Father in heaven is the Lord Jesus Christ.

Consequently, this Scripture passage is a direct reference to the Messiah. In this divine encounter, King David was shown that the Messiah had been appointed by God to serve as a priest forever, according to the Order of Melchizedek. Right there and then, King David knew that there was a higher priesthood available to him than just the earthly priesthood of Levi, which excluded him from participating in the priesthood of God because he was born into the tribe of Judah. That said, the above passage of Scripture shows us some of the spiritual dynamics or experiences we can expect if we stand on the altar of Melchizedek, which is in heaven. Namely:

- God will give us the power to place the enemies of Jesus, the Messiah, under our footstool. Since we are the Body of Christ, we are His feet in the earth, and we're going to trample upon the works of the enemy, based upon the finished work of Christ on the Cross.
- If we stand on the altar of Melchizedek, which is in heaven, God will cause us to rule out of Mount Zion, in the midst of our enemies, both here on earth and in the second heaven, where demonic principalities are located.
- Finally, we are told that if we stand on the altar of Melchizedek, God will renew our youthfulness, instill in our hearts the willingness to

serve Him, and give us the ability to demonstrate His supernatural power here on earth.

It is no wonder the devil doesn't want you to be connected to the heavenly altar of Melchizedek. Without any contradiction, if we are properly aligned to the altar of Melchizedek, we will win the battle of altars each and every time!

The Living Altar of Melchizedek in Heaven

And I saw in the right hand of Him who sat on the throne a scroll written inside and on the back, sealed with seven seals. ²Then I saw a strong angel proclaiming with a loud voice, "Who is worthy to open the scroll and to loose its seals?" ³And no one in heaven or on the earth or under the earth was able to open the scroll, or to look at it. ⁴So I wept much, because no one was found worthy to open [a]and read the scroll, or to look at it. ⁵But one of the elders said to me, "Do not weep. Behold, the Lion of the tribe of Judah, the Root of David, has prevailed to open the scroll and [b]to loose its seven seals." ⁶And I looked, [c]and behold, in the midst of the throne and of the four living creatures, and in the midst of the elders, stood a Lamb as though it had been slain, having seven horns and seven eyes, which are the seven Spirits of God sent out into all the earth. ⁷Then He came and took the scroll out of the right hand of Him who sat on the throne.

(Revelation 5:1-7)

Finally, the above passage of Scripture shows us the exact location of the living Altar of Melchizedek. Once again, it's Saint John, the revelator, to whom this mystery is unveiled.

John was caught up in the Spirit on the day of the Lord. He was given incredible visions of God. In one of these heavenly visions, he was taken to the very throne of God. He saw God, the Father seated on the throne with an ancient scroll in His hand. The scroll was sealed with seven seals. Then out of nowhere, an angel began to proclaim with a loud voice, *"Who is worthy to open the scroll and to loose its seals?"* For a short, frightening moment, there was silence in heaven since no one on earth could open the scroll with the seven seals or even take a look at it. John knew intuitively that whatever was in the scroll was very important to the destiny of men here on earth. He began to weep profusely. Suddenly, one of the 24 elders comforted him and told him, *"Do not weep. Behold, the Lion of the tribe of Judah, the Root of David, has prevailed to open the scroll and to loose its seven seals."*

When one of the elders had identified who was worthy to open the scroll, suddenly, the prophetic vision of John the Beloved shifted to a Lamb. The Lamb was standing before the throne of God as though it had been slain. It had seven horns and seven eyes, which represent the seven spirits of God.

ဆဆဆဆ

The living altar of Melchizedek in heaven is located in the midst of the throne of God. This is why it is the highest altar in all of creation.
ဆဆဆဆ

One day, when I was studying the Bible and saw this passage, the Holy Spirit said to me, "Francis, you have just located the exact location of the living altar of Melchizedek here in heaven." The Spirit of God showed me that the living Altar of Melchizedek is located in the midst of the throne of God. That is why it is the highest altar in all of creation. What altar can be more superior to an altar that functions from the throne room of God in heaven? That is why the devil doesn't want you to understand the Order of Melchizedek, nor to be connected to the living altar of Melchizedek. He is afraid that you might have an unfair and supernatural advantage over him in the battle of altars – and you will! Glory be to God.

PRAYER OF ACTIVATION!

"Heavenly Father, I ask for the Court of Heaven to be seated and for the books of my destiny to be opened as I come before the Judge of all the earth to plead my case against any evil altar in my life or bloodline that is speaking against me. I decree and declare that the Holy Spirit is my official guide and counselor in this courtroom. Heavenly Father, I surrender all rights to self-representation; instead, I ask my defense attorney and mediator of the new covenant, the Lord Jesus Christ, to represent me in your Royal Courtroom against all idols and evil altars that are controlling my life and bloodline, in any way. I also ask the Lord Jesus to heal me by His blood from all soul wounds caused by idols and evil altars in my bloodline. I am seeking a verdict of release from the power of these evil altars in Jesus' Name.

I now enter a plea of 'guilty' into the court's records concerning any legitimate accusations that Satan has filed in Court against me or my bloodline. For Jesus said, in Matthew 5:25, *"Come to terms quickly [at the earliest opportunity] with your opponent at law while you are with him on the way [to court], so that your opponent does not hand you over to the judge, and the judge to the guard, and you are thrown into prison."* Lord, since I am under oath, I cannot lie about my sinful activities and the iniquities of my bloodline that are connected to idolatry and the erecting evil altars. I repent for all sins and transgressions that I and my ancestors ever committed against you and the laws of nature. I repent for not recognizing the order of Melchizedek as the priesthood of the Lord Jesus Christ. Cleanse me from all sin by the blood of Jesus, according to 1 John 1:9. I now formally submit my guilty plea and repentance to the court, in Jesus' Name."

Heavenly Father,

- I decree and declare that I am supernaturally aligned to the altar of Melchizedek in heaven, in Jesus' Name!
- I decree and declare that the altar of Melchizedek is a perfecting altar, which is perfecting everything concern me and my bloodline, in Jesus' Name!
- I appeal to the voice of the blood of the slain lamb at the altar of Melchizedek to speak destiny over my life in Jesus' Name!
- I decree and declare that as I stand on the altar of Melchizedek, the Holy Spirit is giving me the power to place Satan under my feet, in Jesus' Name!
- I decree and declare that as I stand on the altar of Melchizedek, the Holy Spirit is giving me the power to rule in the midst of my enemies, in Jesus' Name!
- I decree and declare that I am completely healed from all soul wounds, which were separating me from the altar of Melchizedek, in Jesus' Name!
- I decree and declare that as I stand on the altar of Melchizedek, the Holy Spirit is renewing my youth like that of an eagle, in Jesus' Name!

LIFE APPLICATION
SECTION

Memory Verse

Now if perfection [a perfect fellowship between God and the worshiper] had been attained through the Levitical priesthood (for under it the people were given the Law) what further need was there for another and different kind of priest to arise, one in the manner of Melchizedek, rather than one appointed to the order of Aaron? 12 For when there is a change in the priesthood, there is of necessity a change of the law [concerning the priesthood] as well. 13 For the One of whom these things are said belonged [not to the priestly line of Levi but] to another tribe, from which no one has officiated or served at the altar.

(Hebrews 7:11-13)

Reflections

1. What is the priestly line of Levi?

2. Why is the altar of Melchizedek the highest altar in all of creation?

End Notes

Chapter 3

[1] Defining API: https://en.wikipedia.org/wiki/API

Chapter 4

[1] https://www.lifenews. com/2020/01/10/61628584-babies-have-been-killed-in-abortions-since-roe-v-wade-in-1973/

[2] rtl.org/multlicultural-outreach/black-abortion-statististics/

Chapter 6

[1] https://lancewallnau.com/alter-altar-break-curse/

Chapter 10

[1] https://www.latimes.com/archives/la-xpm-1994-10-17-ca-51308-story.html

[2] https://youtu.be/km5R3KixDzo (Nicki Minaj explains alter-ego, Roman)

[3] https://en.wikipedia.org/wiki/Baphomet

[4] article on Baphomet from Christianity.com

[5] Beyonce Knowles https://youtu.be/BtTlFW9_sTI (explains alter-ego, Sasha)

Other Resources by the Author

_B_elow are just a few titles you will want to add to your library by Dr. Francis Myles. They can all be found on Amazon.com or on his website, Francismyles.com. His teachings can also be found on YouTube.

Idols Riot (with Katie Souza)

Issuing Divine Restraining Orders from the Courts of Heaven (with Robert Henderson)

The Order of Melchizedek

God Speaks to the Earth

Why God Hates Open Borders

The Joseph of Arimathea Calling

He also offers online schools and coaching sessions. Visit his website for more information.

About the Author

Dr. Francis Myles

In 1989, near the point of death, Dr. Myles had a divine encounter with Jesus Christ. After this powerful healing encounter, Dr. Myles was anointed with a strong gift of healing and prophecy. As a result, he has seen thousands of people healed through his crusades and meetings.

Known as a great "revelator," Dr. Myles has been gifted with biblical insight and revelation into many hidden mysteries of the Word. He is most well-known for his revelation of the Order of Melchizedek. This revelation has resulted in the creation of "The Order of Melchizedek Supernatural School of Ministry," where he has graduated thousands of students worldwide who have learned the life-changing principles of living as "kings and priests" under this powerful Order.

Dr. Myles is a world-renowned author of many life-changing books such as *The Order of Melchizedek,* and *Issuing Divine Restraining Orders from the Courts of Heaven,* to name just a few. He has made several appearances on TBN, GodTV, and Daystar Christian TV networks. He has been a featured guest on Sid Roth's "Its Supernatural TV show, and This Is Your Day with Benny Hinn."

Dr. Francis Myles is also the founder of Marketplace Bible™ International, the creator of the world's first digital Marketplace Bible, which is designed to help millions of Christians around the world to "apply timeless biblical principles to today's marketplace." He is happily married to the love of his life, Carmela Real Myles. Together they reside in McDonough, Georgia, a suburb of Atlanta.

JOIN US EVERY SUNDAY MORNING!

Please visit: *francismyleschurchonline.com*

Its FINALLY HERE... the Vision of Francis Myles Church Online is finally a REALITY! Join us Every Sunday @ 9:30am Eastern Standard Time at our church online website, as well as on our YouTube Channel!